ANCHORED AT
THE ANCIENT, WALLED
HARBOR OF RHODES.

books designed with giving in mind

Crepes & Omelets
Microwave Cooking
Vegetable Cookbook
Kid's Arts and Crafts
Bread Baking
The Crockery Pot Cookbook
Kid's Garden Book
Classic Greek Cooking
The Compleat American
   Housewife 1776
Low Carbohydrate Cookbook

Kid's Cookbook
Italian
Cheese Guide & Cookbook
Miller's German
Quiche & Souffle
To My Daughter, With Love
Natural Foods
Chinese Vegetarian
Jewish Gourmet
Working Couples

Mexican
Sunday Breakfast
Fisherman's Wharf Cookbook
Ice Cream Cookbook
Hippo Hamburger
Blender Cookbook
The Wok, a Chinese Cookbook
Cast Iron Cookbook
Japanese Country
Fondue Cookbook

from nitty gritty productions

This book is lovingly dedicated to
Glenn and Mom who gave me so much help.

THE PARTHENON
ON THE ACROPOLIS

CLASSIC GREEK COOKING

by
DAPHNE METAXAS

Illustrated by **MIKE NELSON**

© Copyright 1974
Nitty Gritty Productions
Concord, California

A Nitty Gritty Book*
Published by
Nitty Gritty Productions
P.O. Box 5457
Concord, California 94524

*Nitty Gritty Books - Trademark
Owned by Nitty Gritty Productions
Concord, California

Library of Congress Cataloging in Publication Data

Metaxas, Daphne.
   Classic Greek cooking.

   1. Cookery, Greek. I. Title.
TX723.5.G8M47   641.5'9495   74-13560
ISBN 0-911954-31-7

TABLE OF CONTENTS

SAILING BY
~SANTORINI~

A CULINARY CRUISE

Greece is a country of varied cuisines. The recipes in this book represent the four corners of Greece and were handed down to me by my four grandparents, who came to America from these various parts of the country. CLASSIC GREEK COOKING is an authentic blend of the four cooking styles of Greece—Athenian, Aegean, Macedonian and Spartan—ranging from every day family meals to holiday specialties.

The recipes I have chosen are those which best represent the traditional, regional cooking of Greece; those most preferred by American tastes (although none have been altered to cater to these tastes); and recipes which do not require a great deal of involved preparation. It is the Greek seasonings and preparation which turn simple, inexpensive ingredients into culinary delights. Most of the ingredients called for are readily available in supermarkets, although a few do require a special trip to a Greek or international grocery store or gourmet shop.

A true sampling of Greek cooking and a peek at the people, their customs and their glorious islands await you on the following pages. I hope you have a delightful experience with all of them.

Daphne Metaxas

GREEK COOKING INGREDIENTS

CHEESES

Feta ("feh-tah")–a crumbly, white cheese made from goat's milk and stored in brine. It is comparatively fat-free and comes in 3 varieties: <u>mild</u>, the least sharp and smoothest in texture; <u>regular</u>, the most widely sold, smooth in texture and a bit salty; and <u>sharp</u>, which is drier and saltier. Feta is sold in delicatessens, supermarkets, gourmet shops, and in Greek and Italian grocery stores. Rinse it in cold water to remove excess brine and refrigerate in a covered container.

Kasseri–a hard, yellow-white table cheese, rich in a flavor all its own. Hard rind should be removed before using. Kasseri is sold in Greek and Italian grocery stores.

Kefaloteri–A hard, salty, grating cheese . . . much like Parmesan. Sold in Greek grocery stores.

Mezithra–A hard, salty, grey-white table cheese. Sold in Greek grocery stores.

OLIVES

Calamata – a speciality of the city of Calamata, Greece. These blackish-maroon olives are probably the most delicious of all Greek olives. They are always split, have pointed tips and a meaty, solid texture. After being soaked in oil and vinegar, they are put into jars. Sold in delicatessens and Greek grocery stores.

Smooth Black – these are the olives most frequently seen in delicatessens. They are round, black and come soaked in brine. Their texture is meaty and soft. They are also sold in supermarkets, gourmet shops, Greek and Italian grocery stores.

Shriveled Black – these are the same as the smooth black olives, only they are farther along in the brining process. They have a shriveled, shiny, black skin, a drier texture, and saltier taste. Sold in Greek and Italian grocery stores.

Extra-Shriveled Black – same as the above only much more shriveled, saltier, drier, and bitter. Sold in Greek and Italian grocery stores.

Cracked Green – these are smooth green olives that have been cracked and marinated in a crock of olive oil, vinegar, salt, garlic and red pimentoes. Somewhat bitter in taste. Sold in Greek and Italian grocery stores.

HERBS AND SPICES

Anise – used in ouzo and in baking.

Allspice, Cinnamon and Nutmeg – these 3 spices are combined in very small amounts to produce a flavor known as Kapama. Used with beef, lamb, chicken and pilaf.

Cumin – used with beef.

Dill – usually used with lamb. In Greek cooking, dill must always be fresh.

Mahlepi – a Persian spice used in making sweet breads. It can be bought in Greek and Middle-Eastern pastry shops and must be finely ground before using.

Mint – spearmint – used in its dry form to flavor ground beef dishes.

Oregano – the most often-used herb in Greek cooking. To get the right flavor from oregano, place the dry leaves on the heel of your left, upturned palm; hold this hand over whatever food is being seasoned. Use the heel of your right hand to finely grind the leaves with back and forth movements.

Pignolia Seeds or Pine Nuts—these are the seeds from a special kind of pine tree and are used in pilafs to add a mild, nutty flavor. They are sold in most supermarkets, gourmet shops and Greek or Italian grocery stores.

Sesame Seeds—used generously in baked goods and pastries.

OTHER

Bulguri—cracked bulgar wheat kernels used to make a nutty-flavored pilaf. Sold in health food stores, supermarkets, and in Greek grocery stores.

Chickpeas—also called garbanzo beans. They are a large, pea-shaped bean with a nut-like flavor. The canned ones are used in soups and stews. Dry-roasted chickpeas are found in Greek grocery stores and they are used as an appetizer nut.

Fides—a fine noodle used in soups and pilaf. Very similar to thin egg noodles.

Filo—("fee-low")—sometimes spelled "phyllo." It is a tissue-thin, buttery dough used in Greek pastries and pittes. Filo can be bought in gourmet shops and Greek and Lebanese grocery stores.

Grapevine Leaves–are soaked in brine and used to make Stuffed Grapeleaves. They are sold in supermarkets, delicatessens, and Greek or Middle-Eastern grocery stores.

Orzo–small, rice-shaped macaroni used in soups or baked with meat stock. Sold in supermarkets, and Greek or Italian grocery stores.

Salonika Peppers–the Greek version of Italian hot peppers. Salonika peppers are mildly hot and make a refreshing appetizer. Sold in jars in delicatessens, supermarkets, gourmet shops and Greek grocery stores.

Tarama–deep, salmon-colored, carp roe caviar used to make a flavorful appetizer dip. Must be refrigerated. Sold in 10 oz. jars in Greek grocery stores.

Turkish Coffee–used to make Greek Coffee. This powder-fine coffee comes from either South America or Africa. Sold in gourmet shops, coffee stores and Greek or Middle-Eastern grocery stores.

WINES AND LIQUORS

Ouzo – a clear, anise-flavored, high-proof liquor made from raisins, fennel and anise seeds. Ouzo, usually served as an aperitif, is clear when served plain and cloudy when ice is added to it.

Cognac – buy the 7-Star variety and serve it after dinner with Greek Coffee.

Retsina – a white wine lightly flavored with pine resin. A favorite in Greece but a flavor for which one must develop a taste.

Rodytis – a rose wine

Kokkinelli – a red, rose wine

Rihea – a dry rose wine

Mavrodaphne – a sweet, Madeira-like wine served either before or after dinner.

PICTURESQUE WINDOW
SEEN IN MANY VILLAGES

APPETIZERS

Appetizers are an essential part of every Greek dinner and are always accompanied by a glass of ouzo or wine. Since breakfast and lunch in Greece are light meals and dinner is served late, appetizers afford the chance to relax and converse with family and friends. A typical family meal begins with a wedge of cheese, olives and cucumber sticks. Sunday or company meals include a wider selection of hot and cold appetizers, many of which are eaten with the fingers.

APPETIZER PLATTER

Amounts needed here will vary with the number of people being served.

feta cheese
kasseri cheese
mezithra cheese
cucumbers cut lengthwise into sticks
tomato wedges
olives: Calamata, smooth black, etc.
Salonika peppers
anchovy fillets
artichoke hearts marinated in lemon and oil
Stuffed Grapeleaves, page 43
Greek Meatballs, page 49

Arrange appetizers on a large platter or individual serving dishes. Ouzo and goblets of water are traditionally served with these appetizers which are eaten with the fingers.

Prepare fillings first.

<u>Cheese Filling</u>:
1 egg, well beaten
1/4 lb. dry cottage cheese
1/4 lb. feta, crumbled
dash of pepper

11

Mix ingredients together. Cover and set aside.

<u>Meat Filling</u>:

1 tsp. finely minced onion	1 tsp. tomato paste
1 tsp. butter	1 tsp. parsley
1/2 lb. lean ground beef	salt and pepper to taste

Saute onion in butter. Brown meat until pink is gone. Mix in remaining ingredients. Cover and chill one hour.

continued

Pastry Triangles continued

Shrimp or Lobster Filling:
1/2 lb. frozen or canned shrimp or lobster
1 large cabbage leaf
1 stalk celery, peeled
1 tsp. butter

1/2 tsp. parsley
1/4 tsp. MSG
salt and pepper to taste

12   If seafood is frozen, cook according to package directions. Drain and dice. Set aside. Boil cabbage and celery until tender. Drain. Squeeze out excess water. Chop. Saute in butter. Add to shrimp. Mix in spices. Cover and chill.

Chicken Filling:
1 tbs. butter
2 tbs. diced celery
2 tbs. chopped onion

1 cooked, diced breast of chicken (or two 5 oz. cans)
1 tsp. minced, fresh parsley
salt and pepper to taste

Melt butter. Saute celery, onion and chicken. Add remaining ingredients. Chill.

Pastry:

1/4 lb. butter, melted   1 lb. filo pastry leaves   fillings

When all fillings are prepared, brush two cookie sheets with butter. Cut filo into lengthwise thirds—Diagram 1. Cover two thirds with a smooth (not terrycloth) damp towel to retain moisture. Filo dries out quickly, so work with speed. Brush top strip of filo with butter. Place heaping teaspoon of filling on the end of the strip—Diagram 2. Fold the lower corner over the filling to make a triangle—Diagram 3. Then fold upper corner straight to the left to make the next triangle—Diagram 4. Continue folding from side to side until the entire strip is used and forms a triangle. Place on cookie sheet, one inch from the edge. Repeat until all filo strips are filled. Bake in 350°F oven 15 minutes or until golden brown. Serve hot. Pastry Triangles freeze well. To reheat, place frozen triangles on cookie sheet. Bake, uncovered, at 350°F about 15 minutes.

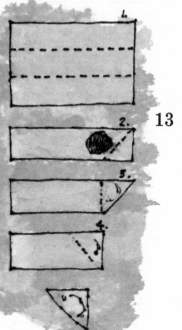

13

TARAMA CAVIAR DIP
Makes 1-1/2 cups

Jars of tarama carp roe caviar can be bought at any Greek grocery store.

2 slices white bread
5 oz. tarama carp roe caviar, at room temperature
juice of 1-1/2 lemons
1 small onion, finely minced
1/2 cup olive oil

Trim crusts from bread. Soak bread in water. Squeeze out excess. Place bread, tarama, lemon juice and onion in blender container (or electric mixer). Blend at medium speed for one minute or until smooth. With blender running add 1/4 cup oil in a slow, thin stream. Repeat with remaining oil. Allow to chill well and thicken before serving. Serve with crackers, or warm, crusty bread for dipping. Mix tarama dip with equal parts of mayonnaise for a delicious salad dressing.

MARINATED LIVER SQUARES
4 - 6 Servings

1 lb. beef liver
juice of 2 lemons
1 tsp. oregano
1/4 tsp. salt
2 dashes pepper
flour
2 tbs. olive oil
1 tbs. butter
lemon

15

Peel and devein liver. Cut into 1 inch squares. Place in bowl. Blend lemon juice, oregano, salt and pepper. Pour over liver. Stir gently. Cover tightly. Marinate for 3 to 4 hours at room temperature. Remove from marinade. Coat each liver square with flour. Fry in mixture of hot oil and butter until crispy-brown. Drain on paper towels. Sprinkle with lemon juice. Serve hot with food picks.

SHRIMPS WITH LEMON SAUCE
4 servings

1 lb. frozen shrimp
1/4 cup fresh lemon juice
1/4 cup olive oil
salt to taste
pinch of oregano

16   Cook shrimp according to package directions. Chill. Beat lemon juice, oil and spices until creamy. Chill 2 hours. When ready to serve, beat lightly. Serve in small bowl surrounded by shrimp. Serve with food picks for dipping.

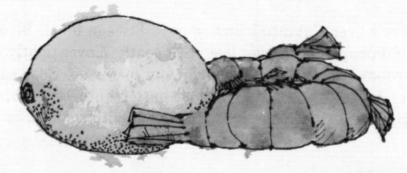

DRY-ROASTED CHICKPEAS WITH RAISINS

1 lb. dry-roasted, salted chickpeas (stragallia)
1/2 lb. currant raisins or golden raisins
<u>OR</u>
1 lb. dry-roasted, unsalted chickpeas (stragallia)
1/2 lb. dark raisins

Toss either combination of ingredients together. Serve in candy dish along with dried, Calamata crown figs as an accompaniment to ouzo. To be eaten with fingers.

17

9TH CENTURY VASE

FRIED EGGPLANT STICKS WITH CREAMY GARLIC DIP
4 - 6 servings

Creamy Garlic Dip:
3 medium potatoes (1-1/2 cups, mashed)
6 - 8 garlic cloves
1/4 cup olive oil
1 tbs. fresh lemon juice
1-1/2 tsp. salt
2 dashes pepper
1/4 cup chicken broth

18

Peel, quarter and boil potatoes in unsalted water. Drain and mash. Peel garlic. Press or mince finely. Place in large bowl. Mash into a juicy pulp with bottom of teaspoon. Add mashed potato. Blend with a fork. Beat in oil, a few teaspoons at a time, until completely absorbed by potatoes. Mix in lemon juice, salt and pepper. Add chicken broth, a little at a time. Continue blending to a smooth, creamy consistency. Serve at room temperature with fried eggplant sticks. Makes almost 2 cups.

Fried Eggplant Sticks:
1 medium eggplant
3/4 cup flour
1/2 tsp. salt
1/4 cup olive oil
1/4 cup vegetable shortening

Peel eggplant. Cut into lengthwise strips 1/4 inch thick, 1 inch wide, and 3 or 4 inches long. Generously sprinkle both sides with salt. Put strips in a colander. Weight them down with several plates. Allow bitter juices to drain out for an hour. Roll strips in combined flour and salt. Heat oil and shortening together. Fry strips over medium-high heat until crispy and golden brown. Drain on paper towels. Arrange around a bowl of Creamy Garlic Dip. Use forks to dip sticks in sauce.

FISHING NEAR KASSIOPI
ON THE ISLAND OF
CORFU

SOUPS

Best known of all Greek soups is Avgolemono, a rich chicken and orzo soup made extra creamy and slightly tart with a frothy blend of eggs and lemon juice.

Other favorite soups like Lamb and Vegetable, Meatball, Lentil and Chickpea are often served as a main course with cheese, crusty bread and a salad.

Trahana Noodles, which look like cracked bits of dried dough and taste delicious, are used in Greek soups instead of pasta or rice.

21

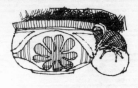

AVGOLEMONO SOUP
4 servings

1 can (46 oz.) chicken broth
1 cup orzo macaroni or 1/2 cup long-grain rice
salt and pepper to taste
2 eggs
juice of 2 lemons

22   Bring broth to a boil. Stir in orzo, salt and pepper. Bring to a second boil. Cover and simmer for 10 minutes or until orzo is tender (20 minutes for rice). Remove from heat. Separate eggs. Beat whites until peaks form. Add yolks. Beat until blended. Add lemon. Stir only until barely mixed. Gently stir two ladlefuls of soup into egg mixture. Pour this combined mixture back into the soup pot. Stir gently. Ladle into soupbowls. Serve immediately, before the froth subsides. Serve before a main course or with crusty bread, cheese and a salad.

MEATBALL SOUP, AVGOLEMONO
8 servings

6 cans (13-3/4 oz. ea.) chicken broth
1 lb. ground beef
1 egg
1 cup long-grain rice
2 tsp. parsley

1 tsp. salt
1/4 tsp. pepper
4 eggs
juice of 4 lemons

Bring broth to a gentle boil in large pot. Combine beef, egg, 1/2 cup rice, parsley, salt and pepper in a bowl. Mix thoroughly with your hands. Form into small balls the size of a nickel. Gently drop balls, one by one, into boiling broth. Add remaining rice. Cover. Simmer **20** minutes or until rice is tender. Remove soup from heat. Make avgolemono: Separate eggs. Beat egg whites until peaks form. Add yolks. Beat until blended. Beat in lemon juice. Stir two ladlefuls of broth into bowl of avgolemono. Then pour mixture back into the soup pot. Stir gently. Serve immediately, before the froth subsides, with crusty bread, cheese and a salad.

23

LAMB AND VEGETABLE SOUP
8 - 10 servings

2 - 3 lamb shanks
1 tbs. butter
1 large onion, chopped
Tops of 1 bunch celery, chopped
3 carrots, sliced
1 onion, quartered
1/4 cup parsley
1 tbs. oregano
1 bay leaf
salt and pepper to taste

1/2 can (6 oz.) tomato paste
3 carrots, thinly sliced
3 stalks celery, sliced
3 - 4 leeks, thinly sliced
1/2 cup lentils, rinsed
1 tbs. salt
1/4 tsp. pepper
2 vegetable boullion cubes
2/3 cup orzo

Trim fat from shanks. Cut meat from bones into bite-sized chunks. Save bones. Melt butter in large pot. Brown meat. Add chopped onion. Saute until golden. Add 6 cups boiling water and bones. Simmer, covered, 2-1/2 hours. In another pot, Combine celery tops, carrots, onion, parsley, oregano, bay leaf, salt, pepper and 8 cups boiling water. Simmer, covered, 2-1/2 hours. Remove bones from lamb stock when done. Discard after taking off any bits of meat. Lift lamb chunks out of stock with slotted spoon. Strain stock through cheesecloth into large pot. Strain vegetable stock through cheesecloth into same pot. Discard cooked vegetables. Refrigerate. When ready to use, skim congealed fat from broth. Bring to a gentle boil. Add remaining ingredients except orzo. Simmer, covered, 10 minutes. Add orzo. Simmer 20 minutes longer. Adjust seasonings. Serve with crusty bread.

LENTIL SOUP
4 - 6 servings

1 lb. lentils
8-1/2 cups water
1 tbs. oil
1 medium onion, chopped
1 can (6 oz.) tomato paste
2 beef boullion cubes
1 tbs. parsley
1 tsp. salt
pepper to taste

Place lentils in large pot. Add water. Bring to a boil. Skim off foam. Simmer, covered, 20 to 30 minutes until lentils are tender. In a separate pan, saute onion in oil. Add to lentils. Mix in tomato paste, boullion, parsley, salt and pepper. Bring to a boil. Simmer, covered, 10 minutes more. Adjust salt. Serve with fresh parsley, wine vinegar or some of each sprinkled on top, and small onion wedges and bread on the side. Bite into the onion, add a spoonful of soup, bite into the bread, then chew. Freezes well.

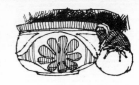

1-1/2 lbs. firm, fresh fish (halibut, cod, perch etc.)
4 cans (8 oz. ea.) minced clams, undrained
1 can (6 oz.) tomato paste
4 - 5 medium potatoes, peeled and diced
2 medium onions, chopped
5 stalks celery, sliced
3 carrots, thinly sliced
1 can (16 oz.) tomatoes, undrained and crushed
1 tsp. oregano
salt and pepper to taste

Rinse fish. Place in pot with 6 cups boiling water. Cover. Simmer over low heat 20 minutes or until tender. Lift fish from pot. Cool. Remove all skin and bones. Cut fish into 1-inch pieces. Set aside. Strain fish stock through cheesecloth. Bring to a boil. Add remaining ingredients. Cover. Simmer 20 minutes or until vegetables are tender. Just before serving, add fish pieces. Heat to serving temperature. Serve with crusty bread.

CHICKPEA SOUP
4 servings

3 cans (16 oz. ea.) chickpeas (garbanzo beans), undrained
1 medium onion, minced
1 cup water
2 beef boullion cubes
1 can (6 oz.) tomato paste
1 tsp. oregano
1/4 tsp. pepper
salt to taste

Combine all ingredients in a sauce pan. Heat to boiling. Cover. Simmer 1 hour. Adjust salt. Serve with crusty bread and a salad. Freezes well.

EASTER SOUP
10 servings

This soup is traditionally served before Easter dinner.

1 honeycomb tripe
1 lb. lamb or calf liver
4 cans (13-3/4 oz. ea.) beef broth
1 bunch dill weed, finely chopped
1 small bunch scallions, finely chopped

2-1/2 tsp. salt
1/4 tsp. pepper
2 cups long-grain rice
6 eggs
1 cup fresh lemon juice

Boil tripe and liver in 3-1/2 quarts water. Skim foam as it forms. Simmer, covered, 2 to 3 hours. Remove from heat. Cool and dice. Strain stock through muslin or cheesecloth into large pot. Add beef broth. Bring to a boil. Add diced meat, dill, scallions, salt and pepper. Simmer 15 minutes. This may all be done ahead of time and refrigerated. One hour before serving, add rice. Simmer until tender, about 20 minutes. Remove soup from heat. Prepare avgolemono: Separate eggs. Beat whites until peaks form. Add yolks. Beat until blended. Stir in lemon juice. Gently stir three ladlefuls of broth into avgolemono. Pour the mixture back into the soup pot. Stir gently. Serve immediately. Freezes well.

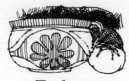

TRAHANA NOODLE SOUP
4 servings

Trahana noodles look like cracked bits of dried dough and are used in soups just like pasta or rice. They come in 3 flavors—sweet, made with milk; sour, made with yogurt or a combination of the two called sweet-sour. Homemade ones are the best, but good ones can be purchased in Greek grocery stores.

Trahana Soup:

3 cans (13-3/4 oz. ea.) chicken broth
1-1/2 cups trahana
salt and pepper to taste

2 eggs
juice of 2 lemons

Bring broth to boil. Stir in trahanas, salt and pepper. Cover. Simmer 10 minutes or until trahanas are tender. Remove from heat. Make avgolemono: Separate eggs. Beat whites until peaks form. Beat in yolks. Add lemon. Beat slightly. Gently stir 2 ladlefuls of soup into avgolemono. Pour mixture back into soup pot. Stir gently. Ladle into soup bowls. Serve immediately, before froth subsides, with crusty bread, cheese and a salad.

Trahana Noodles, Sweet-Sour:

2 eggs, slightly beaten

1/2 tsp. salt

1/2 cup yogurt, whipped with a fork

1/2 cup milk

2 cups farina (cream of wheat)

1 cup flour

In a bowl, blend together eggs, salt, yogurt and milk. Gradually add farina. Add enough flour, a little at a time, to form a stiff dough. Knead 5 minutes. Divide into golf ball sized pieces. Roll into balls. Place on a clean tablecloth or napkin. Completely flatten out with the heel of hand. Let dry overnight. Next day, break each piece into smaller pieces. Turn and continue drying. When completey dry, crush into rice-sized pieces with a rolling pin. Place on baking sheet. Bake in a 140°F oven for several hours until thoroughly dried out. Cook immediately or store in airtight jars. Trahanas keep indefinitely. To make sweet trahanas, use 1 cup of milk with no yogurt. To make sour trahanas, use 1 cup of yogurt and no milk.

SPONGE SELLER
—ATHENS—

BEEF

Beef is rarely served plain in Greece. Instead it is put into rich, tomato stews; layered, lasagna-like between vegetables or macaroni; rolled into balls or "sausages;" or stuffed into grapeleaves, peppers, cabbage and other vegetables. Spices used in cooking beef may seem unusual, but their subtle combinations are surprisingly delicious. Allspice, cinnamon and nutmeg; mint; oregano and cumin are used sparingly with tomato sauce, onions, garlic and wine for intriguing flavors.

PA POU METAXAS' BEEF AND BULGURI CASSEROLE
4 servings

2 lbs. stewing beef
6 tbs. butter
1 large onion, chopped
1 can (6 oz.) tomato paste
salt to taste

1/4 tsp. pepper
1 cup cracked bulgar wheat
1 tsp. salt
1 cup plain yogurt (optional)

34   Cut meat in 1-1/2 inch cubes. Melt 2 tablespoons butter in heavy, 3 quart pot. Brown meat. Add onion. Saute until soft. Add 3-1/2 cups water, tomato paste, salt and pepper. Bring to boil. Cover and simmer 1 hour. This can be done ahead. In another pan, melt remaining butter. Add cracked wheat and salt. Saute over medium heat, stirring constantly to coat all kernels. Add to meat. Bring to a boil. Cover and simmer 30 minutes. Remove from heat. Allow to stand, covered, 15 minutes before serving. Serve with a salad and pass a bowl of yogurt to top the bulguri.

MOM'S PASTITSO
10 servings

Pastitso is the Greek version of lasagna. It consists of layers of elbow macaroni, parmesan cheese and a spicy meat filling, all held together by a rich cream sauce.

Meat Layer:
1 tbs. butter
1 medium onion, chopped finely
3 lbs. ground beef
1 can (6 oz.) tomato paste
1-1/2 tsp. salt

1/4 tsp. pepper
2 tbs. allspice
1 tsp. nutmeg
1 tsp. cinnamon
2 eggs, well beaten

Heat butter in frying pan. Saute onion. Add meat. Saute until pink is gone. Stir in tomato paste, 3/4 cups water, salt, pepper and spices. Cover. Simmer 5 minutes. Uncover. Simmer another 5 minutes. Remove from heat. Adjust salt to taste. Refrigerate. When cool, remove congealed fat. Mix in eggs. Set aside.

continued

Pastitso continued

Macaroni Layers:

1-1/2 lbs. elbow macaroni

2 eggs, well beaten

1 cup grated Parmesan cheese

1/2 cup butter

Cook macaroni according to package directions. Drain well. Put half of macaroni in bowl. Add eggs. Mix thoroughly. Spread in an 11 x 14 x 2 (or similiar) baking pan. Sprinkle with 1/2 cup Parmesan. Spread meat mixture over macaroni. Arrange remaining macaroni over meat layer. Sprinkle with remaining 1/2 cup Parmesan. Melt butter. Pour over Parmesan layer. Top with cream sauce.

Cream Sauce Layer:

4 eggs

3/4 cup milk

1 cup grated Parmesan cheese

1 tbs. flour

1/2 tsp. salt

nutmeg

Beat eggs to a froth. Blend in milk, cheese, flour and salt. Pour over meat-macaroni layers. Sprinkle lightly with nutmeg. Cover with aluminum foil.

Bake in 400°F oven 15 minutes. Remove foil. Bake 45 minutes longer or until golden brown. Remove from oven. Wait 15 minutes before cutting pastitso into squares. Serve with tossed salad.

Pastitso freezes well. Defrost before reheating in 400°F oven 20-30 minutes.

WAGON
IN FARM YARD
STILL USED TODAY

BEEF STEW WITH WINE (STIFADO)
6 - 8 servings

2 lbs. lean stewing beef
1 can (16 oz.) toamtoes
3 tbs. butter
2 lbs. small boiling onions
1/2 cup dry red wine
1/2 tsp. wine vinegar

1/2 can (6 oz.) tomato paste
1/4 tsp. allspice
1/4 tsp. cinnamon
1 tsp. salt
1/4 tsp. pepper

38

Cut meat in 2-inch cubes. Pour tomatoes in bowl. Squeeze to crush into small pieces. Heat butter in a large Dutch oven. Brown meat on all sides. Remove from pot. Set aside. Add onions to pot. Glaze with the butter. Brown very slightly. Remove to a bowl. Cover and set aside. Return meat to pot. Stir in tomatoes, 2 cups water, wine, vinegar, tomato paste, spices, salt and pepper. Bring to a boil. Cover and simmer 1-1/2 hours. Add onions. Cook 30 minutes more or until meat and onions are tender. Serve with crusty bread for sauce sopping.

BEEF STEW, KAPAMA
4 servings

2 lbs. stewing beef
2 tbs. butter
1 medium onion, chopped
3 or 4 medium potatoes
1 can (6 oz.) tomato paste
1/4 tsp. allspice

1/4 tsp nutmeg
1/4 tsp. cinnamon
2 tsp. salt
1/4 tsp. pepper
2 packages (10 oz. ea.) frozen
   French-style green beans, defrosted

39

Cut meat in 1-1/2 inch cubes. Heat butter in a large pot. Brown meat on all sides. Add onion. Saute until soft. Add enough water to just cover beef (about 6 cups). Bring to a boil. Cover. Simmer 1 hour and 15 minutes. This can all be done the night before to save time. Skim off congealed fat before reheating. Peel potatoes. Cut into eighths. Add to meat with tomato paste, spices, salt and pepper. Simmer 20 minutes or until potatoes are almost done. Add green beans to stew. Simmer 10 minutes or until done. Adjust salt to taste. Serve with crusty bread for sauce sopping.

−LINDOS−
THE SEA IS SO
BLUE AND CLEAR

NOODLES WITH KAPAMA MEAT SAUCE
4 servings

1 lb. ground beef
1 tbs. butter
1 can (6 oz.) tomato paste
1/2 tomato paste-can water
2 tsp. allspice
dash of nutmeg and cinnamon
salt and pepper to taste
1 lb. thin egg noodles
Parmesan cheese

41

Saute meat in butter until pink is gone. Stir in tomato paste, water, spices, salt and pepper. Cook, covered, over low heat 10 minutes. Stir frequently. While sauce cooks, boil noodles. Drain. Pour sauce over noodles. Sprinkle with Parmesan. Serve with tossed salad.

NOUNA'S STUFFED CABBAGE ROLLS
4 - 6 servings

1/4 cup butter	1 can (6 oz.) tomato paste
2 medium onions, chopped	1 cup long grain rice
2 lbs. ground beef	1 large cabbage
salt and pepper to taste	3 eggs, separated
1/2 cup dried mint leaves, crushed	juice of 3 lemons

42   Melt butter in skillet. Brown onions. Add meat, salt, pepper and mint. Saute until meat loses its color. Mix in tomato paste and 1 cup water. Simmer, uncovered, 15 minutes. Add rice. Simmer 5 minutes. Cut core from cabbage. Carefully remove leaves. Parboil 10 leaves at a time until limp. Drain carefully. Line bottom of large Dutch oven with the outer leaves. Stuff the remaining leaves by placing a teaspoon of filling in the center of each. Fold stem to the middle, covering filling. Fold left side to the middle. Then fold right side. Tightly roll leaf. Place rolls in concentric layers in the Dutch oven. Add water to just cover rolls. Weigh down with a large plate. Simmer, covered, 30 minutes. Remove plate. Simmer, uncovered, 30 minutes. To make avoglemono sauce, beat egg whites until peaks form. Add yolks. Beat in lemon juice. Pass with cabbage rolls.

STUFFED GRAPELEAVES
6 servings

Called either "yaprakia" or "dolmas," these grapeleaves, rolled around meat and rice filling, make a meal-in-one dinner when served hot and a delicious appetizer or picnic meal when served at room temperature.

1-1/2 lbs. ground beef
2 cups raw, long-grain rice
1 medium onion, finely chopped
3/4 cup olive oil
3 tbs. crushed, dried mint
1 tsp. salt
1 tsp. pepper
1 can (6 oz.) tomato paste
1 jar (2 lbs.) grapevine leaves in brine
1 large lemon
2 eggs
juice of 2 fresh lemons

43

continued

Stuffed Grapeleaves continued

Combine the first 8 ingredients in a large bowl. Use hands to mix thoroughly. Remove first two rolls of grapeleaves from jar. Unroll. Rinse in cold water. Drain. Line the bottom of a 3-quart pot with 3 or 4 leaves. Arrange pot, leaves to be filled and filling within reach on your work surface. Lay a leaf, vein side up, with stem pointing towards you. Place teaspoon of filling on the part of leaf where stem begins. See diagrams. Cover filling with the bottom two points of the leaf.

44

Tuck in side edges. Roll up tightly. Place in bottom of pot. Continue to fill pot with stuffed leaves. Place them tight together in concentric circles, layer upon layer. When pot is full, slowly pour in enough cold water to barely cover stuffed leaves. Squeeze the juice of 1 large lemon over this. Find a sandwich plate or saucer that fits inside of the rim of the pot. Use it to weigh down the leaves so they won't unroll. Cover pot. Bring to a slow boil. Simmer about 1-1/2 hours or until the rice is tender. Add more water as necessary. When done, remove from heat. Let set in covered pot 15 minutes before serving while you make avgolemono sauce: Separate eggs. Beat whites until stiff. Add yolks. Beat until blended. Beat in lemon juice just until mixed. Ladle sauce over servings of Stuffed

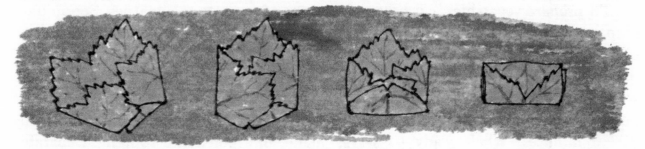

Grapeleaves. Yogurt may be served with "dolmas" if desired. Stuffed Grapeleaves freeze well. When ready to use, defrost first. Then place in saucepan with water to just cover the bottom. Gently steam until heated through. Make fresh avoglemono to pour on top.

STUFFED PEPPERS, TOMATOES OR ZUCCHINI
4 servings

6 - 8 green peppers, or
8 - 9 large, firm tomatoes, or
5 - 7 medium zucchini
1 lb. ground beef
1/2 cup raw, long-grain rice

1 medium onion, chopped
1/4 cup olive oil
1 can (6 oz.) tomato paste
1 tbs. dried, crushed mint
1 tsp. salt

1/4 tsp. pepper
juice of 3 lemons
2 eggs

46 To prepare vegetables, cut holes in the tops of peppers & tomatoes. Scoop out pulp and seeds. Cut off both ends of zucchini. Remove center seed area with a blunt dinner knife. Combine the next 8 ingredients. Mix thoroughly with hands. Stuff into peppers, tomatoes or zucchini. Arrange in baking pan. Add 1 cup water. Sprinkle with the juice of 1 lemon. Cover pan loosely with foil. Bake peppers and zucchini in 400°F oven 1-1/2 hours. Bake tomatoes in 350°F oven 30-40 minutes. When ready to serve, make an avgolemono topping: Separate eggs. Beat whites until peaks form. Add yolks, beat until blended. Blend in the juice of two lemons. Pass sauce with stuffed vegetables.

Freeze. Defrost. Bake at 400°F 30 minutes. Serve with freshly made avgolemono.

HOT FLAT-BREAD SANDWICHES
6 servings

feta cheese, cut into chunks
3 tomatoes, coarsely chopped
1 bunch scallions, including stems, chopped
1 green pepper, coarsely chopped
1 cucumber, peeled, seeded and coarsely chopped
1 tbs. olive oil
1 large onion, chopped

2 lbs. ground beef
6 tbs. catsup
5 tbs. water
1 tsp. allspice
dash of cinnamon
salt and pepper to taste
12 loaves Flat-Bread page 139   47

Place cheese and each vegetable in separate bowls for serving. Heat oil in a heavy saucepan. Saute onion until soft. Add meat. Saute until pink is gone. Drain off excess fat. Mix in catsup, water, spices, salt and pepper. Simmer, uncovered, 5 minutes. Warm bread in 300°F oven. Put warm bread and meat in dishes. Arrange with bowls of cheese and vegetables. Each person slits his own bread along one side and fills it with meat and choice of accompaniments. Flat-Bread sandwiches are to be eaten out of hand.

EVZONES
-ATHENS-

GREEK MEATBALLS
4 servings

4 slices white bread
1 lb. ground beef (or 1/2 lb. ground lamb and 1/2 lb. ground beef)
1 egg
1 medium onion, chopped finely
1 tbs. crushed, dried mint, dill weed or oregano
salt and pepper to taste
flour
2 tbs. butter
2 tbs olive oil

Trim crusts from bread. Place in mixing bowl. Cover with small amount of water. Gently squeeze bread to drain excess water. Return bread to bowl. Add meat, egg, onion, mint, salt and pepper. Mix well with hands. Shape into 2 inch patties. Coat well with flour. Fry patties over high heat in mixture of butter and oil. Turn once. Drain on paper towels. Serve with any flavor pilaf and a hot vegetable. These freeze well. Defrost when ready to use. Reheat in aluminum foil at 400°F for 20 minutes or add to spaghetti sauce.

EGGPLANT MOUSSAKA
6 servings

2 eggplants, 1-1/2 lbs. each
1-1/2 lbs. ground beef
2 tbs. butter
2 medium onions, chopped
1 can (6 oz.) tomato paste
3 tbs. water
2 tbs. chopped parsley

1 tsp. allspice
1/4 tsp. pepper
2 eggs
1/2 cup Parmesan cheese
6 tbs. dry bread crumbs
salt and pepper to taste
Moussaka Sauce, page 51

Peel eggplants. Slice into rounds 1/2 inch thick. Sprinkle both sides generously with salt. Place in deep bowl. Cover with cold water. Place dinner plate on top to keep slices submerged. Let set 1 hour at room temperature. When ready to use, thoroughly rinse and drain. Saute meat in butter until color is gone. Add onion. Cook until soft. Drain off fat. Mix in tomato paste, water, parsley, allspice and pepper. Simmer, uncovered, until liquid is absorbed. Cool 30 minutes. Beat eggs to a froth. Stir into meat. Add Parmesan, 3 tablespoons bread crumbs, salt and pepper. Butter a 13 x 9 x 2 inch baking dish. Sprinkle remaining bread crumbs on bottom. Arrange one third of eggplant slices over crumbs. Cover with half of meat mixture. Add another layer of eggplant and the remaining meat. Top with eggplant slices. Pour Moussaka Sauce over all. Bake in 375°F. oven 1 hour. Remove from oven. Allow to stand 10 minutes. Cut into squares. Serve with a big tossed salad.

Moussaka Sauce:

1/4 cup butter
2 tbs. flour
2 cups milk

4 eggs
1/2 cup Parmesan cheese

1/2 tsp. salt
dash pepper

Melt butter in saucepan over medium heat. Stir in flour until absorbed. Remove from heat. Slowly stir in milk. Cook over medium heat, stirring constantly until mixture thickens and comes to a boil. Remove from heat. Beat eggs 5 minutes. Add a small amount of sauce to eggs. Stir egg mixture back into sauce. Add remaining ingredients. Use in casserole as directed.

Zucchini Moussaka - Use 4 pounds zucchini, sliced 1/4 inch thick. Do not soak.

BEEF AND POTATO MOUSSAKA
6 - 8 servings

7 medium potatoes
1 tbs. olive oil
1 large onion, chopped
1 garlic clove, minced
1-1/2 lbs. ground beef
1 can (6 oz.) tomato paste

1 tomato paste-can of water
1/4 cup chopped parsley
1 tsp. crushed, dried mint
1/2 tsp. cinnamon
1 tsp. salt
1/4 tsp. pepper

Sauce, page 53

Peel potatoes. Slice 1/8 inch thick. Place in a bowl of cold water. Heat oil in saucepan. Saute onion and garlic. Add meat. Brown until pink is gone. Drain off fat. Add tomato paste, water, spices, salt and pepper. Simmer, uncovered, 5 minutes. Butter a 3 quart oblong or similiar baking dish. Drain potatoes. Arrange half the slices in bottom of buttered pan. Sprinkle lightly with salt and pepper. Pour half of sauce over potatoes. Spread meat mixture over sauce. Layer remaining potatoes over meat. Sprinkle with salt and pepper. Pour remaining sauce over all. Bake in 375°F oven 1 hour or until potatoes are tender and top is browned. Cut into squares. Serve with salad and a vegetable. Freeze in foil. Thaw and bake at 400° about 20 minutes.

Sauce:
4 large eggs
1/4 cup butter
1/4 cup flour
2 cups milk
1/2 tsp. salt
dash of pepper
1/2 cup grated Parmesan cheese

53

Beat eggs to a slight froth. Melt butter in heavy saucepan. Stir in flour until absorbed. Remove from heat. Gradually stir in milk. Cook over medium heat, stirring constantly until mixture thickens and comes to a boil. Remove from heat. Stir a small amount of sauce into beaten eggs. Stir mixture back into the saucepan. Blend in salt, pepper and cheese. Use in Beef and Potato Moussaka as directed.

MEATBALL AND VEGETABLE CASSEROLE
4 - 6 servings

1 can (16 oz.) tomatoes, undrained
1/2 cup water
1/2 can (6 oz.) tomato paste
2 pkg. (10 oz. ea.) mixed vegetables, thawed
1 tsp. oregano or dill weed
1 tsp. instant minced onion
salt to taste
4 slices white bread, crusts trimmed

1 lb. ground beef
1 medium onion, finely chopped
1 egg
2 tbs. oregano or dill weed
1/2 tsp. salt
1/4 tsp. pepper
flour

Squeeze tomatoes to crush into small pieces. Combine with tomato paste, water, vegetables, oregano, onion, salt and pepper. Spread in 13 x 9 x 2 inch baking dish. Soak bread in water. Squeeze out excess. Place in mixing bowl. Add meat, onion, egg, oregano, salt and pepper. Mix well with your hands. Shape into flat patties about 2 inches across. Coat well with flour. Arrange on top of vegetable mixture. Bake in 400 F oven 1 hour. Serve with pilaf.

Freeze in foil, thaw when ready to use; bake at 400°F about 20 minutes.

LIVER KAPAMA
4 servings

1-1/2 lbs. calf liver
1/4 cup butter
2 medium onions, thinly sliced
1 cup water
1/2 can (6 oz.) tomato paste
1 tsp. salt
1 tsp. allspice
1/4 tsp. nutmeg
1/4 tsp. pepper

55

Cut liver in 1-1/2 inch squares. Melt butter in frying pan. Lightly saute liver in hot butter until pink is gone. Add onion. Saute 1 or 2 minutes. Add remaining ingredients. Bring to boil. Simmer, covered, 30 minutes or until liver is tender. Serve with pilaf and a tossed salad.

A BEAUTIFUL SPOT
- SKIROS -

LAMB & PORK

Lamb is the staple meat of Greece and is traditionally served with pilaf. For Sunday dinner and celebrations, a leg of lamb is roasted, but for daily meals, lamb is sauced or made into a stew. Next to the leg, lamb shanks are the best cut as they offer the most meat with the least fat. Lamb sauces and stews come in two varieties. One is a thick version of tangy avgolemono, and the other a spiced, tomato sauce. Spices and accompaniments for lamb include garlic, lemon, dill, oregano, tomato sauce, a sparing combination of allspice, cinnamon and nutmeg, and the flavor of the vegetable that the lamb is cooked with. Pork is not served in great amounts like lamb, but prepared in the Greek tradition it is delicious.

ROAST LEG OF LAMB WITH ORZO
10 servings

5 - 7 lb. leg of lamb	3-3/4 cups orzo macaroni	1/2 tsp. pepper
1 tsp. salt	1 can (6 oz.) tomato paste	Parmesan cheese
1 tsp. oil	2 tsp. salt	plain yogurt

Place lamb, fat side up, in roasting pan. Roast in 325°F oven 35 minutes per pound for medium rare. (If desired, adjust cooking time to suit personal taste.) Thirty minutes before lamb is done, bring 4 quarts of water to a boil. Stir in salt, oil and orzo. Parboil orzo for 5 minutes. Drain in a colander. Rinse in cold water. Drain again. When lamb is done, remove it from pan. Wrap tightly in heavy-duty or doubled aluminum foil. Set aside. Add 6 cups water to roasting pan. Mix well to dissolve all drippings. Mix in tomato paste, salt and pepper. Stir in parboiled orzo. Turn oven up to 425°F. Bake mixture for 30 minutes or until orzo is tender and stock absorbed. Adjust salt. Carve lamb. Serve with orzo and Greek Tossed Salad. Pass Parmesan cheese for sprinkling on orzo, or top it with a dollop of yogurt. Orzo is even better reheated the next day. Wrap leftover orzo and lamb in separate packages of foil. Reheat at 425° for 20 minutes. Freeze, defrost and reheat in the same manner.

SHISH KEBAB
8 servings

5 - 7 lb. leg of lamb
1/2 cup (1/4 lb.) butter
1/2 cup olive oil
1 cup fresh lemon juice
2 tbs. oregano
1/2 tsp. pepper
10 - 12 medium tomatoes, quartered
5 - 6 medium onions, quartered and separated
5 - 6 green peppers, cut into 2 inch pieces
8 - 10 15-inch skewers (double-pronged are best)

It is preferable to have a butcher cut lamb into cubes. Place lamb cubes in a deep bowl. Melt butter with oil, lemon, oregano and pepper. Pour over lamb cubes. Marinate 4-5 hours at room temperature. Skewer lamb, onions, tomatoes and peppers in that order. Roast over hot coals or broil. Baste constantly with the remaining marinade. Turn skewers frequently for even cooking. Serve on a bed of pilaf. The same marinade is excellent for lamb chops, too.

LAMB AND LEEK STEW
2 - 4 servings

2 lamb shanks
1 tbs. butter
1/2 can (6 oz.) tomato paste
1 tsp. salt
pepper to taste
3 or 4 leeks or 2 bunches scallions
1/2 cup orzo macaroni

ATHENIAN COIN

Trim fat from lamb shanks. Cut meat from bones into 1-1/2 inch chunks. Save bones. Melt butter in Dutch oven. Brown lamb on all sides. Add 4 cups water, tomato paste, salt, pepper and bones. Bring to a boil. Cover and simmer 1 hour, 15 minutes. Wash and trim leeks well. Cut into 1/2-inch slices including most of the green part. (If scallions are used, cut into 1 inch slices). Remove bones from pot. Add leeks. Simmer, covered, 15 minutes. Add orzo. Simmer 15 minutes longer. Stir often to prevent sticking. Adjust salt. Serve with crusty bread.

LAMB AND CHICKPEA STEW
4 - 6 servings

3 - 4 lamb shanks
1 tbs. butter
1 large onion, chopped
1 can (6 oz.) tomato paste
1 tsp. oregano
dash of allspice
1 tsp. salt
1/4 tsp. pepper
2 cans (16 oz. ea.) chickpeas (garbanzo beans), undrained

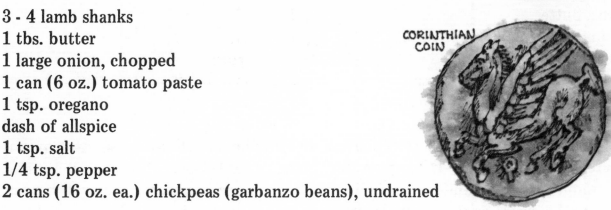

CORINTHIAN COIN

61

Preheat oven to 350°F. Trim fat from lamb shanks. Cut meat into 1 inch cubes. Discard bones. Melt butter in Dutch oven. Brown meat on all sides. Add onions and saute. Stir in 1 cup water, tomato paste and spices. Add undrained chickpeas. Heat to bubbling. Cover. Bake 1 hour. Serve with crusty bread and a salad. Freezes well.

LAMB STEW KAPAMA
2 - 4 servings

2 tbs. butter
2 lamb shanks, fat trimmed off
1 medium onion, chopped
1/2 can (6 oz.) tomato paste
dash allspice, cinnamon & nutmeg

1 tsp. salt
pepper to taste
2 or 3 potatoes
1 package (10 oz.) French cut green beans

62   Heat butter in a large Dutch oven. Brown shanks on all sides. Add onion. Saute until soft. Add 3-1/2 cups water. Bring to boil. Cover. Simmer 1 hour and 15 minutes. (This should be done in advance and refrigerated so fat will harden and can be easily removed.) When ready to finish, peel potatoes. Cut into eighths. Add tomato paste, spices, salt, pepper and potatoes to stew. Simmer 20 minutes or until potatoes are almost done. Add green beans. Simmer 10 minutes or until done. Adjust salt to taste. Serve with crusty bread for sauce sopping.

NOTE: 1 10-ounce package of peas or brussels sprouts or 1 pound fresh zucchini, sliced 1/4 inch thick, may be substituted for green beans. Add zucchini slices along with potatoes.

KAPAMA LAMB AND PILAF CASSEROLE
2 - 4 servings

2 lamb shanks
2 tbs. butter
1 small onion, chopped
1/2 can (6 oz.) tomato paste
1 tsp. allspice
dash of cinnamon

2 tsp. salt
1/4 tsp. pepper
2 tbs. butter
1 cup raw, long-grain rice
1 cup plain yogurt (optional)

63

Trim fat from lamb shanks. In a heavy pot, brown well in butter. Add onions, saute until soft. Add 2-1/2 cups water, tomato paste, allspice, cinnamon, 1 teaspoon salt and pepper. Bring to a boil. Cover and simmer 1-1/2 hours. When lamb is tender melt butter to bubbling in saucepan. Saute rice, stirring constantly, until lightly browned and butter begins to foam between rice kernels. Add remaining salt. Set aside. Remove lamb shanks from pan. Measure broth and add water to measure 2-1/2 cups. Return shanks to pan. Bring to boil. Stir in sauteed rice and butter. Simmer, covered, 30 minutes. Allow to stand, covered, 10 minutes before serving. Pass yogurt to spoon over rice.

SKILLET LAMB CHOPS AND PILAF
2 - 4 servings

2 chicken boullion cubes
1-1/4 cups water
1 tbs. butter
1 garlic clove, finely minced
4 shoulder lamb chops
1/2 cup long-grain rice
1 tsp. salt
juice of 1/2 fresh lemon
parsley
pepper to taste

64

Dissolve boullion cubes in boiling water. Set aside. Melt butter in heavy skillet. Saute garlic. Quickly sear chops over high heat. Pour in boullion. Pour rice around chops. Add salt. Sprinkle with lemon, parsley and pepper. Bring to boil. Cover. Simmer 25 to 30 minutes or until rice is tender and liquid is absorbed. Let stand, covered, 5 minutes before serving.

LAMB SHANKS WITH DILL, AVGOLEMONO
2 - 4 servings

2 lamb shanks
1 tbs. butter
1 tbs. dill weed (1/4 cup fresh)
salt and pepper to taste

1 can (16 oz.) small, whole potatoes
2 eggs
juice of 2 lemons
2 tbs. cornstarch

Trim fat from shanks. Brown well in butter in large Dutch oven. Add 2-1/2 cups water, dill, salt and pepper. Bring to boil. Cover. Simmer for 1-1/2 hours or until lamb is tender and about to detach from the bone. Turn shanks occasionally. Add more water as necessary. Drain potatoes well. Add to shanks. Continue simmering 15 minutes. Adjust salt. Remove from heat. Make thick avgolemono sauce: Beat eggs with whisk until slightly foamy and light yellow in color. Add lemon and cornstarch. Beat once more. Stir a ladleful of lamb stock into the bowl of avgolemono. Gently stir this mixture back into the pot. Cook over medium heat several minutes until thickened. Stir constantly. Serve with lamb shanks and a vegetable. Freeze in plastic containers. Defrost. Reheat, covered, in a saucepan.

LAMB SHANK AND PILAF CASSEROLE
2 - 4 servings

2 lamb shanks
2 tbs. butter
1 garlic clove, finely minced
1 medium onion, chopped
2 tsp. salt
1/4 tsp. pepper

2 tbs. butter
1 cup raw, long-grain rice
4 - 6 tbs. pignolia seeds (pine nuts)
juice of 1/2 fresh lemon
1 tbs. parsley

66

Trim fat from lamb shanks. In heavy pot, brown in butter on all sides, add garlic and onions. Saute until soft. Add 2-1/2 cups water, 1 teaspoon salt and pepper. Bring to boiling. Cover. Simmer 1-1/2 hours. Melt butter to bubbling in a separate pan. Saute pignolias and rice in butter. Stir constantly until butter is light amber in color and begins to foam between the kernels. Add remaining salt. Set aside. Remove shanks from pan. Measure broth. Add enough water, if necessary, to measure 2-1/2 cups. Return shanks to broth. Add lemon and parsley. Bring to a boil. Stir in sauteed rice and butter. Simmer, covered, 30 minutes. Allow to stand, covered, 10 minutes before serving with a crisp, tossed salad.

LAMB SHANKS AND ARTICHOKE HEARTS, AVGOLEMONO

2 - 4 servings

2 lamb shanks
2 tbs. butter
1 medium onion, finely chopped
salt and pepper to taste
1 tbs. parsley

1 can or 1 pkg. frozen artichoke hearts, drained
2 eggs
juice of 2 fresh lemons
2 tbs. cornstarch

Trim fat from lamb shanks. In a large Dutch oven, brown well in butter. Add onion and saute until soft. Add 2-1/2 cups water, salt and pepper. Bring to a boil. Cover, Simmer 1-1/2 hours or until lamb is tender. Turn shanks occasionally. Replenish water if necessary. Add parsley and artichoke hearts. Cook 5 minutes (15 minutes if frozen). Adjust salt. Remove from heat. Make thick avgolemono sauce. Beat eggs with a whisk until slightly foamy. Add lemon and cornstarch. Beat again. Stir a ladleful of lamb stock into the bowl of avgolemono. Gently stir this mixture back into the pot. Stir over medium heat several minutes until sauce thickens. Serve this tasty dish with crusty bread for sauce sopping or on a bed of pilaf. Freeze in plastic containers. Defrost when ready to use. Reheat, covered, in a saucepan.

HIDDEN LAMB
4 servings

Many years ago, Greek guerrilla fighters wrapped and cooked all of their food in parchment paper to prevent enemies from locating their camps by the smell of their cooking. This method of cooking, using aluminum foil instead of parchment, is still used. It is perfect for informal and late arrival dinners, camping, cookouts and picnics.

4 large lamb chops or shanks
1 garlic clove, sliced paper-thin
4 small carrots, cut into 1/2-inch slices
4 small zucchini, cut into 1/2-inch slices
1/4 lb. kasseri cheese, cut into eighths
4 small onions, quartered
4 small potatoes, peeled and cut into eighths
juice of 2 fresh lemons
salt, pepper and oregano to taste
2 tbs. butter

TEMPLE OF APOLLO

Place each lamb chop on an ample length of heavy-duty or doubled aluminum foil. Arrange one fourth of the garlic, vegetables and cheese on top of each chop. Sprinkle with lemon juice and seasonings. Dot with butter. To tightly wrap each package, bring the longest edges of foil together and fold over. Continue folding down until snug against vegetables. Roll and pinch ends to secure. Place the four packages, touching each other, in a baking pan. Bake in 350°F oven 1-1/2 hours. Serve packages on dinner plates to be opened at the table.

SAUCE-BAKED PORK CHOPS AND POTATOES
2 - 4 servings

4 pork chops
2 potatoes, peeled and quartered
1 tbs. oregano
1/4 tsp. garlic powder
salt and pepper to taste
1 can (8 oz.) tomato sauce
1 tomato sauce-can of water

Arrange chops and potatoes in a baking dish. Sprinkle with spices, salt and pepper. Add tomato sauce. Pour water over all. Shake pan gently to mix. Bake in 350°F oven 1-1/2 hours.

CELERY PORK CHOPS, AVGOLEMONO

2 - 4 servings

1 chicken boullion cube
2 tbs. butter
4 pork chops
1 medium onion, finely chopped
3 stalks celery, diced

salt and pepper to taste
1 egg
juice of 1 lemon
1 tbs. cornstarch

Dissolve boullion in 1 cup hot water. Melt butter in frying pan. Quickly sear chops on both sides. Remove from pan. Saute onion and celery until onion is soft. Lay chops on top of onion and celery. Add boullion. Sprinkle with salt and pepper. Cover and simmer 45 minutes. Remove from heat. Make avgolemono sauce: Beat egg until slightly foamy and light yellow. Add lemon juice and constarch. Beat again. Stir a ladleful of pan juices into avgolemono. Gently stir this mixture back into pan. Stir over medium heat for several minutes until sauce thickens. Spoon sauce over chops. Serve with pilaf and crusty bread for sauce sopping.

SEAFOOD IN
OPEN AIR
RESTAURANT
-MIKROLIMANO-

FISH & SEAFOOD

Fish is plentiful in the islands and along the shorelines of Greece. It is eaten often and prepared in many ways. It is always richly flavored using a variety of cooking methods that include marinating in wine, herbs or lemon. Baking fish under mounds of fresh vegetables is a favorite, as is frying. Sauces and toppings are quite often added for variety.

PLAKI
4 servings

Use whatever fish is in season in this baked seafood-vegetable casserole. Besides fish or shrimp, try clams, mussels, scallops or crabmeat.

74

1 can (16 oz.) tomatoes	1 tsp. salt
3 tbs. olive oil	pepper to taste
1 medium onion, chopped	3 stalks celery, chopped
1/2 can (6 oz.) tomato paste	2 carrots, sliced thinly
2 tbs. parsley	*2 lb. fish, head removed
1 tbs. oregano or dill weed	1 lemon thinly sliced

Pour tomatoes in a bowl. Squeeze into small pieces. Heat oil in a pot. Saute onion until soft. Add tomatoes, tomatoe paste, spices, salt, pepper, 1-1/2 cups water and vegetables. Cook, uncovered, until vegetables are tender, about 20 minutes. Pour vegetable mixture into an accommodating casserole or baking dish. Place fish on top. Arrange lemon slices around fish. Bake 35 minutes at 400°F or until tender and flakey. Serve over pilaf.
*or use 2 pounds deveined shrimp. Bake 15 to 20 minutes.

FISH IN WINE AND HERB SAUCE

2 - 4 servings

3/4 cup dry red wine
1 tbs. wine vinegar
2 bay leaves
1/2 tsp. rosemary
4 tsp. tomato paste

1 lb. fish fillets
3/4 cup flour, seasoned with salt and pepper
1/4 cup olive oil
1/4 cup butter
1 small garlic, finely minced

Combine first five ingredients. Set aside. Coat fish in seasoned flour. Allow to stand 5 minutes. Coat with flour again. Set remaining flour aside for later use. Heat oil and butter in a large skillet over high heat. When foam subsides and oil is very hot, add fish. Fry on both sides until crisp and brown. Place fish on plate. Keep warm in 250°F oven. Saute garlic until soft. Add wine mixture. Stir to loosen drippings. Bring to boil. Cook down to thicken. Add flour if necessary. Stir frequently. Pour sauce over fish. Serve immediately with pilaf and a vegetable. For an easy, summertime dish, chill sauced fish for at least 1 hour.

75

BROILED FISH WITH LEMON-HERB SAUCE
4 servings

2 lbs. fish fillets
1/2 cup butter
juice of 2 lemons
1 tbs. oregano, thyme or parsley
salt and pepper

76   Preheat broiler. Arrange fish in "broil and serve" dish. Melt butter in small saucepan. Brush 1 tablespoon over fish. Sprinkle with salt and pepper. Broil until brown and flaky. Add remaining ingredients to melted butter. Blend well and heat slowly. Pour over broiled fish. Serve with pilaf and a hot vegetable.

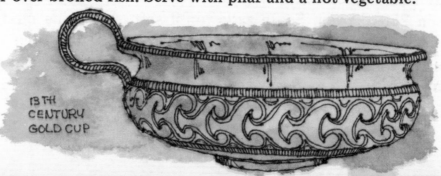

13TH
CENTURY
GOLD CUP

2 lbs. perch, halibut, cod or trout
10 to 12 bay leaves
1/4 cup butter
1/4 cup olive oil
1/2 cup fresh lemon juice
1 tbs. oregano
1/4 tsp. pepper
3 onions, quartered
4 - 6 10-inch skewers

13TH CENTURY VASE

77

Cut fish into 2 inch pieces. Place in deep bowl. Gently mix in bay leaves. Melt butter. Blend with oil, lemon, oregano and pepper. Pour over fish. Marinate 3 to 4 hours at room temperature (less if temperature is over 80°) or overnight in the refrigerator. Skewer onions, fish and bay leaves in that order. Cook over hot coals or under a broiler. Baste and turn frequently. Serve with pilaf.

SHRIMP AND PILAF CASSEROLE
4 servings

1 can (16 oz.) peeled tomatoes
4 tbs. butter
1 cup long-grain rice
1 small onion, finely chopped
2 stalks celery, finely chopped

1 tsp. salt
1/4 tsp. pepper
2 tsp. tomato paste
pinch of garlic powder
1-1/2 lbs. deveined shrimp

78   Empty tomatoes in a bowl. Squeeze into small pieces. In a saucepan, melt 2 tablespoons butter until bubbly. Add rice. Saute until butter is light amber in color and bubbles between the kernels. Do not brown rice. Melt remaining butter in heavy 3 quart pot. Add onion and celery. Saute until tender. Add tomatoes, 1/4 cup water, salt, pepper, tomato paste and garlic powder. Bring to a boil. Simmer, covered until celery is cooked, about 15 minutes. Mix in shrimp. Cook, covered, about 5 minutes or until shrimp turns pink. Add rice. Simmer, covered, 30 minutes. Stir once or twice. Add more water if necessary. Allow to stand 10 minutes before serving.

SHRIMP BAKED WITH FETA, OUZO AND COGNAC

4 servings

1 can (28 oz.) tomatoes
6 tablespoons olive oil
1 medium onion, finely chopped
1 garlic clove, finely minced
1/4 tsp. sugar
salt and pepper to taste

2 tbs. butter
2 lbs. deveined shrimp
3 tbs. ouzo
3 tbs. Metaxa cognac
1/4 lb. feta cheese
2 tbs. fresh, chopped parsley

79

Pour tomatoes into mixing bowl. Squeeze into small pieces. Heat 4 tablespoons oil in heavy saucepan. Lightly saute onion and garlic. Add tomatoes, sugar, salt and pepper. Cook, uncovered, over medium heat until sauce is thickened.

Heat butter and 2 tablespoons oil in large, heavy skillet. Saute shrimp over medium-high heat until pink. Add ouzo and cognac. Flame shrimp. Place in casserole or individual ramekins. Cover with the tomato sauce. Sprinkle with crumbled feta and parsley. (This much of preparation can be done ahead of time.) Bake in 425°F oven 10 minutes or until well-heated and feta has melted. Serve with crusty bread and a salad. Freezes well. Defrost when ready to use. Bake, covered, at 400°F 10-15 minutes.

A BEAUTIFUL VIEW
ON THE ISLAND OF
- KYTHIRA -

POULTRY

For economic reasons, young chickens are seldom used for food in Greece. It is the very mature ones which eventually find their way to the family dinner table in a delicious stew or combined with spices, wine, tomatoes or vegetables, then baked or braised to a delicious tenderness. Avgolemono sauce is a favorite with chicken and pilaf is always on the menu. The recipes which follow have all been adapted to our tender, frying-size chickens.

Greeks of all ages love to play games of all kinds. Here's an old favorite in which a chicken plays a big part.

When a whole wishbone is found at a Greek dinner table, no one makes a wish on it. Rather, it is used to begin a game-of-wits between two people called "Yathis." To begin, the two people who are playing decide on the wager. It can be anything, except money, such as a sweater, a bouquet of roses, a bottle of wine, a service to be rendered, etc. It need not be the same thing for each person. The two players seal their pact by breaking the wishbone together. From now on in order to win, they must follow certain rules when they hand objects to each other. When one player hands the other any object, be it a pencil or a chair, the receiver must, before touching the object, say "I know." If the player forgets to say "I know" and accepts the object, the other person can win the game by immediately saying "Yathis!" (pronounced "yah-thees) which means "Look, I have fooled you!" in Greek.

However if one player hands the other an object and he forgets to say "I know" and the other forgets to say "Yathis!" immediately the game continues. The best "Yathis" games continue for weeks while some have been known to continue for years.

BAKED CHICKEN WITH ORZO
4 servings

1 frying chicken, quartered
1 tbs. butter
1-3/4 cups orzo macaroni
1-1/2 tsp. salt
1/2 tsp. oil

1 cup chicken broth
1/2 can (6 oz.) tomato paste
1/4 tsp. pepper
Parmesan cheese
plain yogurt

Place chicken in a shallow roasting pan, skin side up. Add 1/3 cup water. Dot with butter. Salt and pepper to taste. Bake in 350°F oven 1 hour. Fifteen minutes before chicken is done, bring 2 quarts of water to boil, stir in orzo, 1/2 teaspoon salt and oil. Parboil 5 minutes. Drain orzo in colander. Rinse in cold water. Drain. Remove baked chicken from oven. Place in dish. Cover tightly with heavy-duty foil. Set aside. Turn oven to 425°F. Add 1 cup water and broth to roasting pan. Stir to loosen drippings. Add tomato paste, 1 teaspoon salt, pepper and drained orzo. Bake 30 minutes or until orzo has absorbed liquid and is tender. Adjust salt. Sprinkle orzo with Parmesan cheese or dollops of yogurt. Serve with baked chicken.

83

YIA YIA METAXAS LEMON CHICKEN, OREGANO
4 servings

4 medium potatoes
3 medium onions
1 frying chicken, quartered
1 large lemon
2 tbs. butter
1 tbs. oregano
salt and pepper to taste

84

Peel and quarter potatoes and onions. Place chicken skin side up, in shallow roasting pan. Arrange potatoes and onions between pieces. Add water to cover bottom of pan about 1/2 inch. Squeeze lemon juice over all. Dot chicken and vegetables with butter. Sprinkle with oregano, salt and pepper. Bake for 1 hour in a 350° F oven. Baste occasionally.

Chilled, Lemon Chicken Oregano makes a delicious hot weather meal or chicken salad. Freeze in foil. Defrost and reheat in foil at 400°F 20 minutes.

WINE-BAKED CHICKEN AND ARTICHOKE HEARTS

4 servings

1 frying chicken, quartered
2 cans (14 oz.) artichoke hearts, drained
1 can (15 oz.) tomato sauce
3/4 cup dry sherry or white wine
1/4 tsp. oregano
1 tsp. fresh basil or 1/4 teaspoon dried
pinch garlic powder
salt and pepper to taste

Skin chicken. Place in baking pan. Arrange artichoke hearts around chicken pieces. Combine tomato sauce, wine, spices, salt and pepper. Pour over chicken. Bake in 400°F oven 45 minutes. Baste occasionally. Serve with pilaf and a salad.

SOME WINE GRAPES FROM ONE OF THE ISLANDS

85

MARINATED CHICKEN KEBABS
4 servings

1 frying chicken, quartered
1/4 cup butter
1/4 cup olive oil
1/2 cup fresh lemon juice
1 tbs. oregano
1/4 tsp. pepper
2 - 3 onions, quartered
3 - 4 tomatoes, quartered
4 - 6 10-inch skewers

Skin chicken. Cut meat from bone in 1-1/2 inch pieces. Place in a deep bowl. Melt butter. Blend in oil, lemon, oregano and pepper. Pour over chicken. Marinate 4 to 5 hours at room temperature. (less if temperature is above 80°). Separate onion pieces. Alternate chicken, onion pieces and tomatoes on skewers in that order. Cook over hot coals or under broiler. Baste and turn frequently. Serve with pilaf and a salad.

CHICKEN AND PILAF CASSEROLE
4 servings

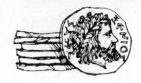

1 frying chicken, quartered
3 tbs. butter
1 onion, finely chopped
1-1/2 cups chicken broth
1/4 tsp. pepper
1 cup long-grain rice
1 tsp. salt
4 - 6 tbs. pignolia seeds (pine nuts)

In a heavy, 3 quart pot, brown chicken in 1 tablespoon butter. Add onion. Saute until soft. Add 1 cup water, broth, salt to taste and pepper. Bring to boil. Cover and simmer 20 minutes. Melt remaining 2 tablespoons butter in another pan. Add rice, salt and pine nuts (pignolia seeds). Saute over medium heat, stirring constantly, until butter foams and is light amber. Add to chicken. Bring to a boil. Cover and simmer 20 minutes. Remove from heat and allow to stand, covered, 10 minutes before serving.

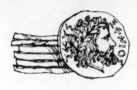

PA POU KARDAS' MEAT, NUT AND PILAF STUFFING
8 servings

This tasty combination makes a delicious stuffing for turkey or chicken, or a side dish with turkey roll or chicken parts, and can be served as a main dish with a vegetable and crisp salad. It is an excellent choice for a buffet dish.

16 - 20 chestnuts
1/4 cup butter
1 cup long grain rice
2 tsp. salt
1/2 tsp. pepper

2-1/2 cups chicken broth
2 pkg. (4 oz. ea.) chopped walnuts
1/4 cup pignolia seeds (pine nuts)
2 lbs. ground beef
1-1/2 tsp. allspice

Cut a deep "X" in each chestnut. Roast in 350°F oven 1 hour. Shell and skin. Melt 2 tablespoons butter in saucepan until bubbly. Add rice, 1 teaspoon salt and 1/4 teaspoon pepper. Saute, stirring constantly until butter is light amber. Add broth. Bring to boil. Cover. Simmer 25 to 30 minutes or until rice is tender and liquid is absorbed. Cool, covered, at room temperature about 30 minutes. Melt 1 tablespoon butter in saucepan. Saute the nuts together about 5 minutes. Melt remaining 1 tablespoon butter in large pot or Chinese wok. Saute beef until pink is gone. Drain off fat. Reduce heat to low. Add allspice, remaining salt and pepper, nuts and cooled pilaf. Mix gently but thoroughly. Use mixture for stuffing or heat gently 2 to 3 minutes and serve as a main dish with or without brown gravy. Freezes well. Defrost and reheat in foil at 400°F 20 minutes.

A HARBOR IN THE AEGEAN

DILLED CHICKEN, AVGOLEMONO
4 servings

1 frying chicken, quartered
1 tbs. butter
1 cup chicken broth
1/4 cup fresh dill weed*, chopped
salt and pepper to taste

2 cans (16 oz. ea.) whole potatoes
2 eggs
juice of two lemons
2 tbs. cornstarch

90   In Dutch oven. brown chicken in butter. Turn skin side up. Add broth, 1 cup water, dill weed, salt and pepper. Bring to boil. Cover. Simmer for 35 minutes. Drain potatoes, add to chicken stock. Continue simmering 15 minutes, or until chicken is done. Remove from heat. Make thick avgolemono sauce: Beat eggs with a whisk until slightly foamy. Add lemon juice and cornstarch. Beat. Stir a ladleful of chicken stock into avgolemono. Gently stir mixture back into the pot. Stir over medium heat until thickened. Serve immediately over chicken. Freezes well.

*1 tbs. dried dill weed

CHICKEN STEW, KAPAMA
4 servings

1 frying chicken, quartered
1 tbs. butter
1 small onion, chopped
1 can (6 oz.) tomato paste
1 tsp. allspice
1/4 tsp. nutmeg
dash of cinnamon

1 tsp. salt
1/4 tsp. pepper
4 potatoes, peeled and quartered
2 pkg. French green beans OR 2 pkg.
peas OR 2 pkg. okra OR 2 zucchini
cut 1/2 inch OR 4 sliced carrots
and 5 stalks celery cut 2 inches

In heavy pot, brown chicken in butter. Add onion. Saute until soft. Turn chicken pieces, skin side up. Add 2 cups water, tomato paste, spices, salt and pepper. Simmer, covered, for 15 minutes. Add potatoes. If using fresh vegetables, add with potatoes. Simmer 30 minutes or until chicken is tender. Defrost frozen vegetables. Add after potatoes have cooked 15 minutes. Simmer, covered, 15 minutes or until chicken is tender. Adjust salt. Serve with crusty bread for sopping.

MAKING DELIVERIES
ON NARROW
STEEP STREETS

PITTA

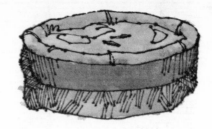

Pitta, pronounced "pea-tah," is a large, main dish pie served on special, festive occasions. It has a flaky, buttery crust filled with meat or vegetables. The most traditional filling is a combination of spinach and feta cheese. Pitta is baked in a deep pan and served in wedges. Pitta's exceptionally flaky crust is made by alternating layers of filo and butter. Filo pastry sheets can be bought in Greek grocery stores and gourmet shops and makes a delecate, super-flaky crust of tissue-thin layers. Follow the basic Pitta recipe for any of the fillings. All filling recipes make enough for two cake pan-sized pittes.

BASIC PITTA
12 servings

Choice of filling (see following pages)
2 8- or 9-inch cake pans
10 tbs. melted butter
1 pkg. (16 ozs.) filo

Prepare filling as directed in the recipe you are using. When ready to make pittas, spread each cake pan with 2 tablespoons melted butter. Separate 12 filo sheets from package. Place under a dampened, smooth (not terrycloth) towel to keep from drying out. Wrap the remaining filo pastry sheets well and freeze. (Filo can be refrozen several times without spoiling.) Brush top filo sheet liberally with melted butter. Fold sheet in half. Brush with more butter. Place doubled sheet in cake pan to line bottom. Let filo edges overlap pan by 2 inches. Repeat buttering, folding and layering until 3 doubled sheets of filo line cake pan. Repeat procedure for second pan. Keep remaining 6 filo sheets covered with the dampened towel. Divide cooled, well-drained filling evenly between the two filo-lined pans. (At this point, the Spinach and Feta filling and the Leek and Feta filling have butter drizzled over them before the top crusts are added. The other fillings do not have butter added. All pittas have butter drizzled over the crusts.) Uncover the remaining 6 filo sheets. Brush top sheet liberally with butter. Fold and butter again. Place on top of filling. Let filo edges overlap pan by 2 inches. Repeat process until 3 doubled filo sheets cover each pan. Brush overlapping filo edges with butter. Press top and bottom crust edges together. Fold over 1 inch. Fold over again 1/2 inch. Continue around the pan to seal and make a thick rim. Drizzle 2-1/2 tablespoons melted butter over each top crust. Make two slits to let steam escape. Bake in 375°F oven 40-50 minutes or until golden brown and flaky throughout. Puncture crust with fork if it puffs. Remove from oven. Let set 10 minutes before serving. Cut each pitta into 6 wedges. Serve hot.

One 12 x 9 x 2 inch pan (or similar) can be used instead of cake pans. Use the same ingredients for 1 large pan as for 2 small ones. Bake 45-50 minutes. Cut in squares and serve.

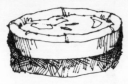

BEEF PITTA FILLING
for 2 pittes

1 lb. ground beef
1 small onion, finely chopped
1/4 cup water
1/2 tsp. salt
1/4 tsp. pepper
2 eggs, slightly beaten

96

Lightly saute meat in frying pan. Add onion, water, salt and pepper. Cook, stirring frequently, until meat is crumbly and no longer pink. Simmer, uncovered, over medium heat until water evaporates, 8 to 10 minutes. Stir occasionally. Adjust salt and pepper. Remove from heat. Cool completely before using. Prepare pitta crusts according to directions given in the basic recipe on page 94. When bottom crusts are in the pans and top crusts are ready, add eggs to cooled filling. Place top crusts over fillings and proceed as directed in basic recipe.

CHICKEN PITTA FILLING
for 2 pittes

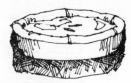

3 tbs. butter
1/2 small onion, finely minced
1 stalk celery, finely diced
3 - 4 cups shredded, cooked chicken
1 tbs. fresh parsley, minced
1/2 tsp. salt
pepper to taste
2 eggs, beaten

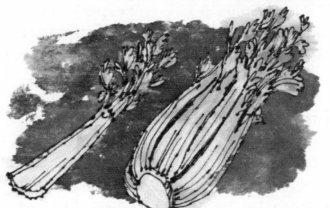

Heat butter in skillet. Saute onion and celery until tender. Add chicken. Lightly saute. Mix in parsley, salt and pepper. Cover. Set aside to cool completely before using. Prepare pitta crusts according to directions given in the basic recipe on page 94. When bottom crusts are in the pans and top crusts are ready, add eggs to cooled filling. Place top crusts over fillings and proceed as directed in basic recipe.

YIA YIA KARDAS' SPINACH AND FETA PITTA FILLING
for 2 pittes

2 lbs. fresh spinach	pepper to taste
2 large eggs	1/2 lb. feta cheese
1 tsp. salt	5 tbs. melted butter

Wash spinach several times in cold water. Drain well. Snap off stems. Squeeze water from a few leaves at a time. Lay leaves on chopping board and slice into thin shreds. Place shreds in colander. Press firmly to squeeze out any remaining water. Pat with paper towels. Repeat until all spinach is shredded. Press all shreds into colander and allow to stand at least 1 hour before using. Prepare pitta crusts according to the directions given in the basic recipe on page 94. When bottom crusts are in the pans and the top crusts are ready, place well-drained spinach in a bowl. Break eggs over it. Sprinkle with salt and pepper. Finely crumble 3/4 of the feta over top and mix ingredients thoroughly. Spread filling in prepared crusts. Sprinkle with remaining feta and drizzle 2-1/2 tablespoons melted butter over each filling. Place top crusts over fillings and proceed as directed in basic recipe. Serve hot or at room temperature.

LEEK AND FETA PITTA FILLING
for 2 pittes

1 dozen medium-sized leeks
2 large eggs
1 tsp. salt

pepper to taste
1/2 lb. feta cheese
5 tbs. melted butter

Fill a large pot 1/4 full with water. Bring to boil. Wash leeks thoroughly in cold water. Discard outside leaves and roots. Use white part of leeks and 3 inches of the green. Cut lengthwise into quarters, then dice. Place in a colander. Rinse thoroughly under cold, running water. Add leeks to boiling water. Cover and simmer 15 minutes. Drain. Cool in colander. Shake off excess water. Allow to stand in colander at least 1 hour before using. Prepare pitta crusts according to directions given in the basic recipe on page 94. When bottom crusts are in the pan and the top crusts are ready, combine well-drained leeks, eggs, salt, pepper and 3/4 of the feta, finely crumbled. Mix well. Spread filling in prepared crusts. Crumble remaining feta over fillings and drizzle 2-1/2 tablespoons melted butter over each filling. Place top crusts over fillings and proceed as directed in basic recipe.

ΦΡΕΣΚΑ ΣΑΝΑΤΥΚΑ

OPEN AIR
VEGETABLE MARKET

VEGETABLES

Greeks love vegetables and serve a wide variety with their daily meals. Artichokes, cauliflower, eggplant, chickpeas, okra, potatoes, green beans, spinach, tomatoes and zucchini are all treated with the same respect as meat. They are fried, stuffed, combined with cheeses and other vegetables, casseroled or stewed with tomato sauce, or served with a refreshing lemon sauce.

AUNT JANE'S FRESH VEGETABLE CASSEROLE
4 - 6 servings

4 tbs. olive oil
3 garlic cloves, thinly sliced
3 large onions, cut into thin rings
3 green peppers, quartered
1 medium eggplant, sliced 1/4 inch
5 small zucchini, sliced 1/4 inch
5 medium tomatoes, thinly sliced
salt and pepper to taste
3 - 4 tbs. fresh, minced basil

102

Heat 3 tablespoons olive oil in Dutch oven. Lightly saute 2 cloves garlic. Add a portion of each vegetable, including the remaining garlic clove, in layers in the order listed. Sprinkle each layer with salt, pepper and basil. Drizzle remaining tablespoon of oil over surface. Cook, covered, over low heat 30 minutes. Gently shake casserole occasionaly to prevent sticking. Remove cover. Cook 5-10 minutes longer to reduce and thicken sauce. Serve hot or chilled.

ARTICHOKES WITH LEMON SAUCE
2 - 4 servings

2 fresh artichokes
1 tsp. salt
1/2 cup fresh lemon juice
1/2 cup olive oil

Wash and trim artichokes. Bring pot of water to boil. Add 1/2 teaspoon salt and artichokes. Cover tightly with foil. Pierce with several small holes to let steam escape. Gently boil until tender. Drain artichokes. Prepare sauce: Combine lemon juice, oil and remaining 1/2 teaspoon salt. Whisk or shake in a jar until smooth and creamy. Serve artichokes whole or cut in half. Place in small, shallow bowls with sauce poured liberally over them.

DEEP FRIED ARTICHOKE HEARTS
3 - 4 servings

2 cans (14 oz.) artichoke hearts
1/2 cup grated Parmesan or kefaloteri cheese
3/4 cup fine, dry bread crumbs
2 eggs
corn oil for deep frying

104   Drain artichokes. Dry on paper towels. Combine cheese and bread crumbs. Beat eggs until frothy. Dip each artichoke heart into beaten egg. Roll in bread crumbs. Dip into egg again. Roll in bread crumbs once more. Deep fry until golden brown. Serve hot.

BEETS WITH CREAMY GARLIC DIP

3 - 4 servings

1 lb. fresh beets or 1 lb. can sliced beets
Creamy Garlic Dip, page 18, at room temperature

   Cut tops from beets, leaving about 2 inches of stem. Wash beets. Drop into boiling, salted water. Cover. Simmer until tender about 20-30 minutes. (Don't test tenderness until beets are almost done as piercing makes them bleed.) When done, rinse in cold water. Slip off skins and slice. (If using canned beets, pour contents of can into saucepan. Heat to boiling. Remove from heat. Drain.) Serve hot beets in individual dishes. Pass Creamy Garlic Dip. Place a dollop on beets.

105

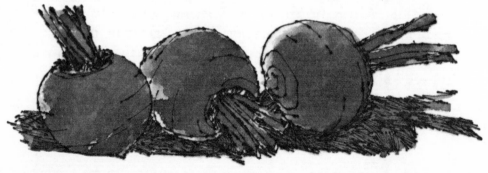

CAULIFLOWER WITH LEMON SAUCE
4 servings

1 medium-head cauliflower <u>or</u>
2 packages (9 oz. ea.) frozen cauliflower
1/4 cup fresh lemon juice
1/4 cup olive oil
1/2 tsp. salt

106   Cook cauliflowerets in a small amount of boiling, salted water about 10 minutes or until tender. Do not overcook. (Prepare frozen cauliflower according to package directions.) Prepare dressing while cauliflower cooks. Combine lemon juice, oil and salt. Whisk or shake well in jar until smooth and creamy. Drain cauliflower. Place in individual serving dishes. Drizzle dressing over. Serve hot. This lemon and oil dressing is also excellent on brussels sprouts, broccoli and spinach. Prepare and serve exactly as for cauliflower.

FRIED EGGPLANT WITH CRISP CHEESE CRUST

4 - 6 servings

1 medium-sized eggplant
oil for frying
1 tsp. butter
4 eggs, well beaten
1 cup crumbled feta or grated kasseri cheese
salt and pepper
fresh parsley

Peel eggplant. Cut into strips 2 inches long and 1/2 inch thick. Generously sprinkle strips with salt. Place in bowl of cold water. Let stand at least 1 hour. Rinse and drain thoroughly. Dry on paper towels. Pour oil in large frying pan to cover bottom. Heat. Add butter. Fry eggplant sticks on one side. Turn. Immediately add eggs, cheese, pepper and a pinch of salt. Cook until eggs are done. Serve, garnished with parsley.

LITTLE EGGPLANTS WITH ONIONS
6 - 8 servings

2 lbs. tiny eggplants
garlic cloves
salt
1 can (16 oz.) tomatoes, undrained
1/2 cup olive oil

4 medium onions, sliced into rings
2 tbs. tomato paste
1 tsp. salt
1/4 tsp. pepper

108   Trim stems from eggplants. Wash well. Cut a small slit in the middle of each one. Insert garlic half in each slit. Arrange eggplants on plate. Generously sprinkle with salt. Let stand 30 minutes. Rinse off salt. Dry on paper towels. Pour tomatoes into small bowl. Break into little pieces. Heat oil in a frying pan. Fry eggplants on all sides until soft and light brown. Remove to saucepan. Fry onion rings in remaining oil until glazed and tender. Add tomatoes, tomato paste, salt and pepper. Simmer, uncovered, over medium heat 15 minutes. Pour over eggplants. Add 2/3 cup water. Bring to boil. Cover. Cook over medium heat 45 minutes. Stir frequently to prevent sticking. Serve immediately.

THATCHED WINDMILLS
OVERLOOKING THE
SEA IN MYKONOS.

GREEN BEAN STEW
4 - 6 servings

2 pkg. (10 oz. ea.) French green beans
4 large potatoes
1 tbs. olive oil
1 small onion, chopped
1 garlic clove, finely minced (optional)
1/2 cup water
1/2 can (6 oz.) tomato paste
2 tsp. salt
pepper to taste

Defrost green beans. Peel potatoes. Cut into eighths. Cover with cold water. Heat oil in large pan. Lightly brown onion and garlic. Add water, tomato paste, salt and pepper. Drain potatoes. Add to sauce. Stir in green beans. Add water to cover vegetables half-way. Cover. Simmer until potatoes are tender, about 30 minutes. Add more water as stew cooks, if needed.

SPINACH WITH LEMON AND FETA

4 servings

3 lbs. fresh spinach
juice of 2 lemons
1/4 cup olive oil
3/4 cup feta cheese, cubed or crumbled
1/4 tsp. each salt and pepper

Wash spinach well. Place in pot. Add 1-1/2 cups water. Cover tightly. Cook over medium heat about 10 minutes. Drain thoroughly. Combine lemon juice and oil. Shake or beat until creamy. Place drained spinach in bowl. Sprinkle with cheese, salt, pepper and dressing. Mix well. Serve hot.

ZUCCHINI BAKED WITH CHEESE
4 - 6 servings

4 small zucchini
oil for frying
2 eggs
1 cup grated Parmesan cheese
dash of pepper

112   Wash and peel zucchini. Cut into 1/2-inch slices. Heat oil in frying pan. Saute zucchini until lightly browned. Drain on paper towel. Arrange slices in oiled baking pan. Beat eggs until frothy. Mix in cheese and pepper. Pour over zucchini. Bake 15 minutes in 350°F oven, or until crust turns golden brown. Serve hot.

ATTIC CUP 6TH CENTURY

CRISP-FRIED ZUCCHINI
4 - 6 servings

4 small zucchini
flour
oil
4 - 6 lemon wedges
Creamy Garlic Dip, page 18

Wash and peel zucchini. Cut into 1/2 inch slices. Sprinkle lightly with salt. Dredge slices in flour. Fry in hot oil, over medium heat until golden and crisp. Arrange hot slices in individual serving dishes. Garnish with lemon wedges. Pass Creamy Garlic Dip. Serve dip at room temperature.

113

VASE IN THE FORM OF A BRIDLED MULE'S HEAD THEY DRANK WINE FROM THE TIP OF THE MUZZLE WHEN UNCORKED. 6TH CENTURY

POTATOES WITH LEMON SAUCE
6 servings

5 large potatoes
1 tbs. salt
juice of 2 lemons
1/2 cup oil
2 tbs. minced parsley
1 small onion, finely minced
salt to taste

Scrub potatoes. Bring a large pot of water to boil. Add salt and potatoes. Cover pot. Boil until almost tender, about 30 minutes. Remove from heat. Let potatoes stand in water, tightly covered, 15 minutes longer. Combine lemon and oil until smooth and creamy. Drain potatoes. Peel and slice into large bowl. Sprinkle with parsley, onion and salt. Drizzle on dressing. Toss well. Add more salt if needed. Serve hot.

POTATOES MOUSSAKA
6 - 8 servings

6 large potatoes
oil for frying
1 medium onion, chopped
1 garlic clove, finely minced
1 can (16 oz.) tomatoes, undrained

1/2 can (6 oz.) tomato paste
2 tbs. minced parsley
1/2 tsp. salt
1 cup grated Parmesan cheese
1 tbs. butter

Peel potatoes. Cut into thin slices. Fry in oil until golden. Drain. Saute onion and garlic until golden. Squeeze tomatoes into small pieces. Add to onion. Stir in tomato paste, parsley, salt and pepper. Simmer, covered, 5 minutes. Uncover. Simmer until sauce thickens, about 15 minutes. Add 3/4 cup cheese. Lightly oil casserole dish. Layer with 1/4 of potatoes and 1/4 of sauce. Continue until sauce and potatoes are used. Sprinkle remaining cheese over top. Dot with butter. Cover. Bake in 350° F oven 30 minutes. Uncover. Bake 15-20 minutes longer.

115

TEMPLE OF APHAEA
-AEGINA-

SALADS

Salads accompany every Greek dinner and range from the classic lettuce salad to combinations like spinach and feta, cucumbers and yogurt, or green beans with tomatoes, onions and feta. Best known is the Greek Tossed Salad—a luncheon meal in itself which combines salad greens with crumbled feta cheese, olives, hot peppers, achovies, oregano and fresh oil and vinegar dressing.

Many other unusual vegetable combinations become favorite salads when tossed with lemon juice or vinegar and olive oil, or yogurt and dill or garlic. Always use olive oil and lemon juice or vinegar in equal amounts.

GREEK TOSSED SALAD
8 servings

1/2 head iceberg lettuce
1/2 peeled cucumber, sliced
1/2 green pepper, cut up
1 tomato, in wedges
2 scallions, chopped
4 radishes, sliced
8 Calamata olives

8 Salonika peppers
anchovy fillets
1/2 cup feta cheese, crumbled
1/2 tsp. oregano
salt and pepper to taste
olive oil
wine vinegar

118

Tear lettuce into bite sized chunks. Toss with next 5 ingredients in a large bowl. Garnish with olives, peppers, anchovies and cheese. Sprinkle oregano, salt and pepper on top. Just before serving, drizzle olive oil, to taste, over the salad. Then sprinkle on vinegar in an equal amount. Toss well. Serve immediately. For a luncheon, serve in large portions with crusty rolls.

BEET SALAD

1 lb. fresh beets or 1 can (16 oz.) sliced beets
1 small onion, chopped
1/4 cup olive oil
1/4 cup vinegar
1/2 tsp. salt

Wash beets and tops. Leave 2 inches of stems on beets. Coarsely chop remaining tops. Drop beets and greens into boiling, salted water. Cover. Simmer until tender, 20-30 minutes. (Don't test tenderness until cooking time is almost up as piercing makes beets bleed.) Drain. Chop stems and greens. Rinse beets in cold water. Slip off skins. Slice into bowl. Add chopped stems and greens. Cool 1 hour. If using canned beets, drain well. Put in bowl. Sprinkle beets with onion. Combine oil, vinegar and salt. Blend. Pour over beets. Mix well. Serve at room temperature.

119

CUCUMBER SALAD
4 servings

1 cup (1/2 pint) plain yogurt
1 tsp. fresh lemon juice
1 tbs. fresh, chopped dill weed
salt to taste
3 medium cucumbers

120   Blend yogurt, lemon juice, dill and salt together in bowl. Chill in refrigerator. When ready to serve, peel cucumbers. Discard end tips. Slice very thin. Gently combine with yogurt mixture. Garnish with dill. Serve immediately.

THE OLD CITY -RHODES-

CHICKPEA SALAD
2 - 4 servings

1 can (16 oz.) chickpeas (garbanzo beans)
1 small onion, finely chopped
2 tsp. minced parsley
1/4 cup olive oil
juice of 1-1/2 lemons
1/4 tsp. salt

Drain chickpeas. Rinse in cold water. Drain well again. Place in bowl. Sprinkle with onion and parsley. Beat oil, lemon and salt until creamy. Pour over chickpeas, mix thoroughly. Serve at room temperature.

EGGPLANT SALAD
6 servings

1 large eggplant
1 medium onion, miced
1 garlic clove, finely minced
4 tomatoes, cut in small wedges
2 - 3 tbs. chopped parsley
salt and pepper to taste
1/4 cup olive oil
1/4 cup white vinegar

Place eggplant in pan. Bake in 350°F oven until soft, about 1 hour. Rinse in cold water. Peel. Dice eggplant. Place in bowl. Allow to cool at room temperature. Chill in refrigerator 1-2 hours. To serve, sprinkle with onion, garlic, tomatoes, parsley, salt and pepper. Beat oil and vinegar until smooth and creamy. Pour over vegetables. Toss. Serve chilled.

GREEN BEAN AND TOMATO SALAD

2 pkg. (10 oz. ea.) frozen French-style green beans*
1 tomato, cut in small wedges
1 small onion, finely chopped
1/2 cup diced or crumbled feta
1/4 cup olive oil
1/4 cup wine vinegar
1/2 tsp. salt
1/2 tsp. oregano

Cook beans according to package directions. Drain well. Cool. Place in bowl. Add tomato wedges, onion and feta. Beat remaining ingredients together. Pour over salad. Mix well. Serve at room temperature.

*or 1 can (1 lb.) green beans, well drained.

GREEK POTATO SALAD
6 servings

1 tbs. salt
5 large unpeeled potatoes, well scrubbed
1 small onion, finely minced
2 tsp. oregano
salt to taste
juice of 2 lemons
1/2 cup oil

124

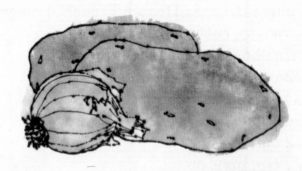

Bring large pot of water to boil. Add salt and potatoes. Cover. Boil until almost tender, about 30 minutes. Remove from heat. Let potatoes stand in water, tightly covered, 15 minutes longer. Drain and peel. Slice into large bowl. Allow to cool at room temperature. Chill in refrigerator 1-2 hours. At serving time sprinkle with onion, oregano and salt. Combine lemon and oil. Beat until creamy. Drizzle over potatoes. Toss and serve.

RAW SPINACH SALAD
4 - 6 servings

1 lb. fresh spinach
1/2 cup diced or crumbled feta
1/4 cup olive oil
juice of 1 lemon
1/2 tsp. salt
pepper to taste

Wash spinach several times. Drain thoroughly. Place in bowl. Sprinkle with feta. Combine remaining ingredients. Beat until creamy. Drizzle over spinach. Toss to mix ingredients. Add more salt if needed. Serve immediately.

WINDMILLS AT ENTRANCE OF THE HARBOR OF RHODES

 **FIVE FAVORITE DRESSINGS**

Cucumber Dressing:

2 medium cucumbers   salt
juice of 1/2 lemon   1 cup (1/2 pint) plain yogurt

Peel cucumber. Discard tips. Cut in half, lengthwise. Scoop out and discard seeds. Dice. Place in mixing bowl. Combine with lemon juice and salt. Stir in yogurt. Chill, covered, overnight. Makes 2 cups.

126

Lemon and Oil Dressing:

juice of 2 lemons   1/4 tsp. oregano
1/2 cup olive oil   salt

Combine all ingredients. Beat vigorously until creamy. Serve over lettuce, cooked broccoli, spinach, cauliflower or brussels sprouts. Store in refrigerator. Makes 1 cup.

Variation: Omit oregano. Add 1 mashed garlic clove.

Lemon and Garlic Dressing:

Follow the recipe for Lemon and Oil Dressing. Omit oregano. Add 1 small garlic clove which has been put through a garlic press, or well mashed.

Yogurt and Dill Dressing:

1 cup (1/2 pint) plain yogurt   2 tbs. fresh, chopped dill weed

Blend ingredients together. Salt to taste. Cover. Allow to stand at room temperature several hours. Refrigerate overnight. Makes 1 cup.

Variation: Substitute finely mashed garlic for dillweed.

Yogurt and Garlic Dressing:

1 garlic clove   1 cup (1/2 pint) yogurt

Peel garlic. Put through press. Thoroughly blend with yogurt. Add salt to suit taste. Cover. Allow to stand 30 minutes before refrigerating overnight.

13TH CENTURY VENETIAN
CASTLE OF METHONI
~MESSINIA~

PILAFS

Pilaf accompanies most meals in Greece as the main starch instead of potatoes. Rice kernels are sauteed in butter then simmered in a rich chicken broth. Pilaf is also often made with cracked bulgar wheat kernels. Seasonings for pilaf include various vegetables, dill, nuts and kapama sauce.

PILAF
4 servings

2 tbs. butter
1 cup long-grain rice
1 tsp. salt
1/4 tsp. pepper
2-1/2 cups chicken broth

130   Melt butter in heavy saucepan over medium heat. Stir in rice, salt and pepper. Saute, stirring constantly, until butter is light amber and foams. Add broth. Bring to full boil. Cover. Lower heat. Simmer 25 to 30 minutes or until rice is tender and liquid is absorbed. Let rice stand, covered, 15 minutes before serving.

PILAF KAPAMA
4 servings

2 tbs. butter
1 cup long-grain rice
2-1/2 cups chicken broth
2 tbs. tomato paste
1 tsp. salt
1/4 tsp. allspice
1/4 tsp. nutmeg
dash of cinnamon
plain yogurt

131

Melt butter in heavy saucepan over medium heat. Stir in rice. Saute, stirring constantly, until butter is light amber and foams. Stir in broth, tomato paste, salt, allspice, nutmeg and cinnamon. Bring to a boil. Cover. Simmer 25 to 30 minutes or until rice is tender and liquid is absorbed. Let stand, covered, 15 minutes before serving. Top servings with yogurt if desired.

PILAF WITH NUTS
4 servings

2 tbs. butter
1/4 cup pine nuts
1/4 cup slivered almonds
1 cup long-grain rice
1 tsp. salt
2-1/2 cups chicken broth

132

Melt butter in a heavy saucepan over medium heat. Add nuts. Saute until lighly browned. Stir in rice and salt. Saute, stirring constantly, until butter is light amber and foams. Stir in broth. Bring to boil. Cover. Simmer 25 minutes or until rice is tender and liquid absorbed. Let stand, covered, 15 minutes before serving.

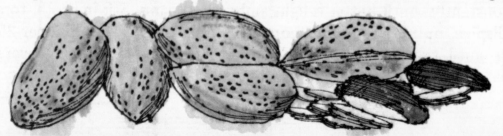

1 lb. green shrimp
2 tbs. butter
1/2 cup celery, finely diced
1 cup long-grain rice
1 tsp. salt
1/4 tsp. pepper
1 tsp. fresh dill (optional)
2-1/2 cups chicken broth

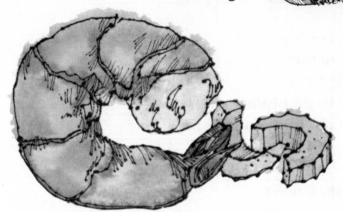

133

Peel and devein shrimp. Melt butter in heavy saucepan over medium heat. Add shrimp and celery. Saute until shrimp turns pink. Stir in rice, salt and pepper. Saute, stirring constantly, until butter is amber. Stir in dill and broth. Cover. Simmer 25 to 30 minutes or until liquid is absorbed. Let stand, covered, 15 minutes before serving.

PILAF AND SPINACH CASSEROLE
6 servings

2 lbs. fresh spinach
1/4 cup olive oil
1 large onion, minced
1 can (6 oz.) tomato paste
3 tomato paste cans of water
1 cup long-grain rice
1 tsp. salt
1/4 tsp. pepper

134

Thoroughly wash spinach. Drain well. Tear leaves in half. Heat oil in a heavy pot. Saute onion until golden. Add tomato paste, water, rice, salt and pepper. Mix well. Bring to boil. Stir in spinach. Cover. Cook over lowest heat 20 to 30 minutes or until rice is tender. Do not lift cover during cooking. Shake pot occasionally to keep spinach from scorching. Serve immediately.

Bulguri is a tasty, nut-like flavored pilaf made from cracked bulgar wheat. This healthful wheat can be bought in Greek grocery stores, gourmet shops, and most supermarkets.

1/4 cup butter
1 cup bulgar cracked wheat
2 tsp. salt
1/4 tsp. pepper
2-1/2 cups chicken broth
1/2 can (6 oz.) tomato paste
plain yogurt

135

Melt butter in heavy saucepan over medium heat. Add bulgar wheat, salt and pepper. Saute, stirring constantly, until butter is light amber and foams. Stir in broth and tomato paste. Bring to boil. Cover. Lower heat. Simmer 30 minutes or until wheat is tender and all liquid is absorbed. Let stand, covered, 15 minutes before serving. Top each serving of bulguri with a dollop of yogurt, if desired.

A GOAT HERD
NEAR VATHI
ON ISLAND OF
-ITHACA-

BREADS, EGGS CHEESE

Bread is extremely popular in Greece. It is found on the Greek table at breakfast, lunch and dinner. In fact, the typical Greek lunch consists of fresh bread, cheese and olives.

There are two main kinds of bread. Those served everyday, such as the well known Greek or Flat Bread and sweet, special occasion treats like Cardomom Butter Braid for New Year's Day and the colorful Anise Braid which is so much a part of the Easter tradition.

GREEK BREAD
makes 2 loaves

1 pkg. dry yeast	1/4 cup shortening	3-3/4 - 4 cups flour
1/3 cup warm water	2 tbs. sugar	3 tbs. melted butter
1 cup milk	1 tsp. salt	

Mix yeast and 105° to 115° water until dissolved. In a saucepan, combine milk, shortening, sugar and salt. Heat. Stir until sugar and shortening are dissolved. Cool to lukewarm. Pour into bowl. Stir in 1 cup flour. Beat well. Add yeast. Beat until smooth. Gradually mix in remaining flour to make moderately stiff dough. Place on floured surface. Knead until smooth and satiny, about 10 minutes. Shape dough into ball. Place in lightly-oiled bowl. Turn to oil all sides. Cover. Put in warm place to rise about 1-1/2 hours or until doubled. Punch dough down. Knead on floured surface 10 minutes. Place in oiled bowl. Cover. Let rise in warm place 1-1/2 hours. Punch down. Place on floured surface. Divide in half. Shape each half into a ball. Let rest 10 minutes. Place dough on greased and floured baking sheet. Brush with melted butter. Let rise, uncovered, in warm place 1 hour or until doubled. Bake in 375°F oven 45 minutes or until golden. Cool slightly before serving.

138

FLAT-BREADS
makes 10 loaves

5 to 5-3/4 cups flour   2 tsp. salt   2 cups very warm water
1 tbs. sugar   1 pkg. active dry yeast

Combine 2 cups flour, sugar, salt and yeast in bowl. Add 120° to 130° water. Beat 2 minutes on medium speed. Add 3/4 cup flour. Beat on high speed 2 minutes. Add flour to make soft dough. Place on floured surface. Knead until smooth and elastic, 8-10 minutes. Place dough in large oiled bowl. Turn to grease all sides. Cover. Set in warm spot. A rack in an unheated oven with a pan of hot water beneath the rack works well. Let rise, about 1 hour or until doubled. Punch dough down. Place on a floured surface. Cover. Let rest 30 minutes. Divide in 10 equal pieces. Shape each into a ball. On floured surface, roll each ball into a 6 inch circle. Place on a lightly floured, ungreased cookie sheet. Preheat oven to 450°F. Slide circles directly onto the floor of hot oven, or put them in a preheated, very hot, iron skillet placed on the lowest oven rack. Bake until done and puffy, about 5 minutes. Place under broiler for a minute to lightly brown. Cool. Slit open. Serve with cheese or make Flat-Bread Sandwiches, page 47. Freezes well. Reheat, without thawing, unwrapped in 400 F oven several minutes.

139

NATIVE COSTUME
AND FOLK DANCING

RED EGGS FOR GOOD LUCK

Hard cooked eggs, dyed red, are a Greek tradition at Easter time. Two or three of these brightly colored eggs are nestled into each Anise Braid before baking. This symbolizes good luck for the household. A favorite family game is for everyone to grasp one of the red eggs tightly in his hand with the point showing. Each tries to crack the other's egg. The winner is the lucky one who successfully escapes having his egg cracked.

EASTER BREAD: ANISE BRAID
makes 1 braid

1 pkg. dry yeast
1/4 cup 105° to 115° water
1/3 cup sugar
1/4 cup butter, softened
1/2 tsp. salt
1/2 cup milk
142 1/4 tsp. oil of anise
5 drops oil of cinnamon
2-3/4 to 3 cups flour
2 eggs
1 tbs. water
3 tbs. sesame seeds

Sprinkle yeast over water, mix until dissolved. In large mixing bowl combine sugar, butter and salt. Heat milk to scalding. Pour over contents of mixing bowl. Stir until butter melts. Let cool to lukewarm. Add anise and cinnamon. Stir in 1 cup flour. Beat well. Add 1 beaten egg and dissolved yeast. Beat well. Gradually mix in remaining flour to make a soft, but not sticky, dough. Place dough on a floured surface. Cover. Let rest 10 minutes. Knead until smooth and elastic, 8-10 minutes. Shape dough into a ball. Place in lightly-oiled bowl. Turn it to grease all sides. Cover and set in a warm place for about 1-1/2 hours until doubled in size. Punch dough down. Cover bowl. Return to warm place. Let rise again until almost doubled again. Place on floured surface, divide into 3 equal parts, shape each part into a ball. Cover. Let rest 10 minutes. Grease a baking sheet and set aside. Use hands to roll each dough-ball into an 18 inch rope, tapering the ends. Line ropes, 1 inch apart, on the baking sheet. Working from the middle to each end, loosely braid the ropes. Be careful not to stretch the dough. Pinch ends together. Tuck them under slightly. Cover. Let rise in warm place about 45 minutes or until doubled in bulk. Beat water and remaining egg together. Brush gently over braid. Sprinkle generously with seasame seeds. Bake in 375°F oven about 25 minutes or until deep brown. Cool slightly before serving.

DAD'S FRIED CHEESE SANDWICHES
1 serving

1 tbs. butter
3-1/2 inch thick slices of kasseri or feta cheese
1 warmed Flat-Bread or 2 slices hot toast

144   Melt butter in frying pan over high heat. Before it bubbles, reduce heat to medium. Place cheese slices in pan. Fry until slightly soft and crispy on one side. Add more butter if necessary. With a wide spatula, carefully flip cheese slices. Let cook a minute. Serve in the pocket of Flat-Bread or in between slices of toast.

ISLAND OF PAROS

GREEK CHEESE OMELET
4 servings

1 tbs. butter
1/4 cup finely diced green pepper
4 eggs
2 tsp. milk
1/2 cup crumbled feta or kasseri
pepper to taste

145

Melt butter in large frying pan. Add green pepper. Saute over a low heat until tender. Remove pan from heat. Lift peppers from pan with slotted spoon allowing butter to remain. Beat eggs and milk until frothy. Mix in cheese, pepper to taste and sauteed peppers. Return frying pan to a low heat. When butter is hot pour in eggs. Turn when set around edges. Cook second side until done. Fold omelet and serve.

NEW YEAR'S BREAD: CARDOMOM BUTTER BRAID
makes 1 braid

This rich cake-bread is traditional for New Year's Day. The cook places a silver coin, wrapped in foil, somewhere in the dough before baking. Before dinner the head of the house cuts a slice for each member of the family naming each slice as he cuts. The slice containing the coin is believed to bring good luck to the recipient for the coming new year. There is also one slice cut for the house, which denotes that the whole household will be happy and lucky for the year.

1 pkg. active dry yeast
1/4 cup warm 105° to 110° water
1/3 cup sugar
1/4 cup butter, softened
1/2 tsp. salt
1/2 cup milk

1-1/2 tsp. whole cardomom seeds*
2-3/4 to 3 cups flour
1 egg, beaten
1 tbs. water
1 egg
3 tbs. sesame seeds

Sprinkle yeast over water. Mix until dissolved. Combine sugar, butter and salt in large mixing bowl. Heat milk to scalding. Pour into mixing bowl. Stir until butter melts. Cool to lukewarm. Crush cardomom seeds with mortar and pestle.

Stir into mixing bowl. Stir in one cup flour. Beat well. Add beaten egg and disolved yeast. Beat well. Gradually mix in remaining flour to make a soft, but not sticky, dough. Place on floured surface. Cover. Let rest 10 minutes. Knead until smooth and elastic 8-10 minutes. Shape dough into ball. Place it in a lightly-oiled bowl. Turn to grease all sides. Cover. Set in warm place 1-1/2 hours or until doubled in size. Punch down. Let rise another hour until almost doubled again. Turn dough onto floured surface. Divide into 3 equal parts. Shape each part into a ball. Cover. Let rest 10 minutes. Grease a baking sheet. Set aside. Use hands to roll each dough ball into an 18 inch rope. Taper ends. Line ropes 1 inch apart, on baking sheet. Working from the middle to each end, loosely braid ropes. Be careful not to stretch dough. Pinch ends together. Tuck them under slightly. Cover. Let rise in warm place about 45 minutes or until doubled in bulk. Beat water and remaing egg together. Brush gently over braid. Sprinkle generously with sesame seeds. Bake at 375°F 25 minutes or until crust is deep, amber brown. Cool slightly before serving with slices of feta cheese. Delicious with coffee.

*1 tbs. ground cardomom or mahlepi (found in Greek pastry shops).

NAFPAKTOS

PASTRIES

Greek cuisine is famous for its rich, sticky, pastries made with chopped nuts, honey-syrup, all manner of spices, and a tissue-thin, buttery flaky dough called filo. It takes much expertise to make this leaf-like dough, but luckily, all Greek groceries and many gourmet food shops carry filo ready for use. Filo can be frozen, thawed, and refrozen several times without spoiling.

Dessert in the Greek home always consists of fresh fruits, nuts and cheese—never pastries. The rich pastries are offered to guests, on holidays and festive occasions and as a special treat between meals. Always serve pastries with cups of Greek Coffee.

BAKLAVA
makes 2 - 3 dozen pieces

3/4 cup finely chopped walnuts
3/4 cup finely chopped pistachio nuts
1/2 cup finely chopped, blanched almonds, toasted
1/2 cup superfine sugar
1 tsp. cinnamon
1 tsp. nutmeg
1-1/4 lb. sweet butter, melted
1 pkg. filo pastry sheets

150

Combine nuts, sugar, cinnamon and nutmeg. Brush a 13 x 9 x 2 baking pan well with butter. Separate 25 filo pastry sheets from package. Place under a smooth (not terrycloth), damp towel to prevent drying. Wrap remaining filo well. Freeze for future use. Place one filo sheet in pan. Trim to fit. Brush generously with melted butter. Repeat procedure until there are 5 layers of buttered filo in the pan. Sprinkle 1/4 of nut mixture over buttered sheets. Butter and layer 5 more filo sheets. Sprinkle with 1/4 of nut mixture. Repeat this procedure two more times, ending with filo. Drizzle any remaining butter over top. Bake in 300°F oven 1-1/2 hours or until golden brown. Remove baklava from oven. Using a sharp knife, immediately cut long, diagonal lines from corner to corner, forming an "x." Follow these guidelines to cut baklava into serving-sized diamonds. While still hot, pour cooled syrup over baklava.

Syrup:
2-1/2 cups sugar
1-3/4 cups water
finely grated rind of 1 orange
finely grated rind of 1 lemon

5 whole cloves
1 cinnamon stick
1 cup honey

Combine sugar, water, orange and lemon rinds, cloves and cinnamon stick in saucepan. Bring to boil. Simmer, uncovered, about 5 minutes to thicken syrup slightly. Remove from heat. Discard spices. Stir in honey. Cool at room temperature. Pour over hot baklava. Allow to stand overnight before serving.

FARINA CAKE
10 - 12 servings

3 cups water
2-1/2 cups sugar
juice of 1/2 lemon
1/2 lb. sweet butter
1 cup sugar

6 eggs, well beaten
1 tsp. vanilla
1 cup flour
1 cup farina (cream of wheat)
3 tsp. baking powder

152   Bring water to boil in a saucepan. Stir in sugar until dissolved. Simmer, uncovered, about 5 minutes or until slightly thickened. Stir in lemon juice. Remove from heat. Cool at room temperature. Cream butter in large mixing bowl. Add sugar. Cream 5 minutes longer. Beat in eggs and vanilla. Add flour, farina and baking powder. Beat until smooth. Pour into buttered 9 x 13 x 2 baking pan. Bake in 375°F oven, about 30 minutes or golden brown. Remove from oven. Immediately cut into squares, using sharp knife. Pour cooled syrup over hot cake. Let set 1 hour before serving.

RICH ALMOND CAKE
makes 3 dozen pieces

1-1/4 cup sugar
1-1/2 cup water
2 tsp. fresh lemon juice
6 eggs, separated
1 cup sugar

3/4 cup blanched almonds, finely chopped
1/3 cup finely crushed zwieback
1 tsp. baking powder
1/2 tsp. almond extract
1/4 lb. sweet butter, melted

In a small saucepan, combine sugar, water and lemon juice. Bring to boil. Simmer, uncovered, 10 minutes or until clear. Cool at room temperature. Do not refrigerate. Beat egg yolks in large mixing bowl until fluffy. Gradually add sugar. Beat well. Fold in finely chopped nuts, zwieback, baking powder and extract. In a separate bowl, beat egg whites until stiff. Gently fold into yolk mixture. Fold melted butter in well. Turn into buttered, 10 x 13 x 2 pan. Bake in 325°F oven 45 minutes, or until top springs back when touched. Pour cooled syrup over hot cake. Cool. Cut into diamonds.

NUT AND COGNAC PASTRY-CAKE
makes 2 dozen pieces

Syrup:

3-1/2 cups water	2 lemon slices	1 cinnamon stick
3 cups sugar	5 whole cloves	
3 orange slices	2 tsp. fresh lemon juice	

Simmer ingredients in saucepan, uncovered, 30 minutes. Strain. Do not refrigerate.

154

Crust:

1-1/2 cups sweet butter	2 tsp. fresh-grated orange rind
1 cup superfine sugar	1-1/2 oz. cognac
2 egg yolks, beaten	1-1/2 to 2 cups cake flour

Butter a 10 x 14 x 2 baking pan. Cream butter. Add sugar. Cream. Beat in egg yolks, one at a time. Stir in orange rind and cognac. Add flour to make a soft dough. Press into pan to cover bottom and up the sides 1/2 inch. Prick with fork. Bake in 350°F oven 15 minutes or until golden.

Filling and Filo Top:

1/2 lb. toasted, blanched almonds	2 tsp. cognac
1/2 lb. walnuts	8 eggs, separated
1 tbs. flour	1/2 cup superfine sugar
1 tsp. baking powder	8 sheets of filo pastry
1 tsp. cinnamon	3/4 cup sweet butter, melted
1 tsp. almond extract	

Finely chop nuts. Mix with flour, baking powder, cinnamon, almond extract and cognac. Beat egg yolks until frothy. Add sugar. Beat until thick and lemon colored. Combine with flour mixture. Beat egg whites until stiff, but not dry. Fold carefully into nut mixture until well mixed. Spread on baked crust. Liberally brush one filo sheet with melted butter. Place it, buttered side up, over cake filling. Repeat until all filo sheets are used. Pour remaining butter over top. Bake in 350°F oven 1 hour or until crust is flaky and light golden. Remove from oven. Immediately cut into diamond-shaped pieces, using a sharp knife. Carefully pour cool syrup over hot cake. Allow to stand 12 to 24 hours before serving.

ORANGE AND SPICE WALNUT CAKE
12 - 15 servings

8 zwieback
1 lb. walnuts
1-1/2 cups sugar
7 eggs, separated
grated rind of 1 orange
1/2 tsp. cinnamon
156 1/2 tsp. nutmeg
1 tsp. baking powder
confectioners' sugar

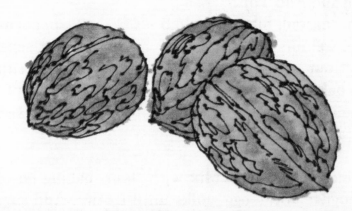

Grind zwieback and walnuts in blender. Mix with sugar. Beat egg yolks until thick. Beat egg whites in large bowl until soft peaks form. Fold yolks into whites, alternately with zwieback mixture. Add orange rind, cinnamon, nutmeg and baking powder. Pour into well buttered 10 x 14 x 2 inch pan. Bake in 425°F oven 15 minutes. Reduce temperature to 275°F. Bake 45 minutes longer. Cake is done when a cake tester inserted in center comes out clean. Cool cake in pan. Cut into squares. Sprinkle with confectioners' sugar.

AN OLD FISHERMAN

LITTLE SPICE AND BRANDY CAKES
makes 3 dozen small cakes

1/2 cup peanut oil

1/4 lb. sweet butter

3 tbs. fresh orange juice

1/4 cup cognac or brandy

1 egg, well beaten

1-1/2 cups flour

1-1/4 tsp. baking powder

1-1/2 tsp. cinnamon

1-1/2 tsp. ground cloves

3/4 cup finely chopped walnuts

1/4 cup sugar

158

Heat oil and butter in saucepan until hot but not boiling. Remove from heat. Mix in orange juice and cognac. Cool. Stir egg into cooled mixture. Sift flour and baking powder together. Add cinnamon and cloves. Mix well. Slowly add flour mixture to egg mixture. Dough should be soft but stiff enough to form a ball that holds its shape. If too soft and sticky, add a little bit more flour. With floured hands, pinch off small portions of dough about 3 inches round. Shape into ovals. Place 1 inch apart on ungreased cookie sheets. Combine walnuts, sugar and dash of cinnamon and cloves. Push a teaspoon of filling into each cake center with your finger. Close dough over the filling. Reshape into ovals. Bake in 425°F oven 25 minutes or until golden brown. Cool. Dip in syrup.

Syrup:

2 cups sugar
1 cup water
1 lb. honey
1 small lemon, sliced
chopped walnuts

159

   Bring the syrup ingredients to boil in saucepan. Simmer, uncovered, 5 minutes until thickened. Remove lemon slices. Dip small cakes in hot syrup with a slotted spoon. Place on cake racks to drain. Sprinkle immediately with chopped walnuts. Allow to stand 4 hours before serving.

EASTER COOKIE TWISTS
makes 4 - 5 dozen cookies

1 lb. sweet butter
1-1/4 cups sugar
6 eggs
1 cup (1/2 pt.) heavy cream

2 tsp. vanilla
3 heaping tsp. baking powder
8 - 10 cups flour
2 cups sesame seeds

160 Cream butter. Add sugar. Cream until smooth. Beat 4 eggs until frothy. Beat into creamed mixture until smooth. Beat in heavy cream. Stir in vanilla and baking powder. Beat to thoroughly blend ingredients. Gradually stir in flour, 2 cups at a time, until dough is soft and pliable. Knead on lightly floured surface 10 minutes until smooth. To test for right consistency for shaping, tear off a bit of dough about 1-1/2 inches in diameter. Using fingers like a rolling pin, roll into a strip 1/2 x 8 inches. Fold strip in half as in Diagram A.

Overlap dough, Diagram B, until a twist is formed, Diagram C. Dough is ready for shaping if it does not crack during process. If it does crack, continue kneading a little longer. When ready, shape dough as in test. Keep unused dough covered as you work to prevent its drying out. Place twists 1 inch apart on buttered baking sheets. Beat 2 eggs with 2 tablespoons water. Brush over cookies. Sprinkle with generous amounts of sesame seeds. Bake in 350°F oven 10 to 15 minutes or until cookies are light golden.

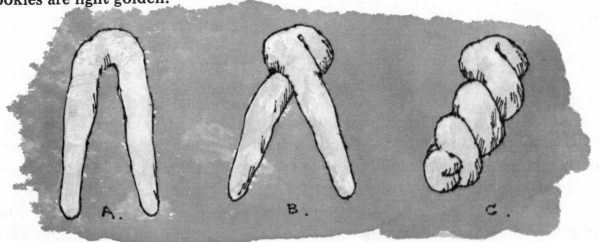

HONEY FRITTERS
makes 2 dozen

1-1/2 cups honey
3 tbs. sweet butter
2 tbs. sugar
1 cup flour
1 tsp. baking powder
4 large eggs
shortening or oil for deep frying
cinnamon

Combine honey and 1/4 cup hot water. Heat 1 cup water to boiling. Add butter. Allow to melt. Lower heat. Add sugar, flour and baking powder all at once. Stir vigorously over low heat until mixture forms a ball. Remove from heat. Cool to lukewarm, about 8 minutes. Add eggs, one at a time. Beat well after each addition. Beat until shiny. Heat shortening, in deep pot with frying basket, to 360°F. (Pot should be half full.) Drop batter by tablespoons into hot fat. Fry until golden brown. Drain on paper towels. Place hot fritters on cake rack. Drizzle honey over tops. Sprinkle lightly with cinnamon. Serve hot.

SHREDDED WHEAT PASTRY
6 servings

3 cups sugar
1-3/4 cups water
2 tbs. fresh lemon juice
1 lb. sweet butter, melted
1-1/2 lbs. shredded wheat crumbs
3 cups finely chopped walnuts
1 tsp. cinnamon
1 tsp. nutmeg

163

Combine sugar, water and lemon juice in saucepan. Bring to boil. Simmer, uncovered, 15 minutes. Cool at room temperature. Butter a 9 x 12 x 2 baking pan. Spread half of shredded wheat in bottom of pan. Drizzle half of butter over it. Mix walnuts and spices. Sprinkle over buttered, shredded wheat. Layer remaining shredded wheat over nuts. Drizzle with remaining butter. Bake in 350°F oven 45 minutes. Remove from oven. Pour syrup over hot pastry. When cool, cut into diamonds.

RICH BUTTER-AND-WALNUT BALLS
makes 2 dozen cookies

1/2 lb. sweet butter
1/4 cup confectioners' sugar
1 tsp. cognac
1/2 tsp. vanilla
2 cups flour, sifted
1-1/2 cups finely chopped walnuts
164 24 whole cloves
confectioners' sugar

PHALANTHUS
ON A DOLPHIN

COIN OF
TARENTUM
5TH CENTURY

Cream butter until light. Add sugar. Continue beating until light. Stir in cognac and vanilla. Gradually add flour. Mix well. Fold in chopped nuts. Shape dough into 2 inch balls. Place on ungreased cookie sheets, 1 inch apart. Insert whole clove in the center of each cookie so that only the crown shows. Bake in 350° F oven 15-18 minutes. Sift confectioners' sugar onto a large piece of waxed paper. While cookies are still hot, place on sugared paper. Sift additional confectioners' sugar over tops and sides. Cool before serving and storing.

– METEORA –

IN OLDEN DAYS VISITORS REACHED
THE MONASTERIES BY ROPE LADDER
OR BY BEING HAULED UP IN A BASKET.

NUT AND PASTRY ROLLS
makes about 2 dozen

Syrup, page 167
1/2 cup walnuts
1/2 cup toasted, blanched almonds
1/2 cup superfine sugar
1/2 tsp. cinnamon
1/4 tsp. ground cloves
1/4 tsp. nutmeg
1 tbs. cognac or brandy
1/2 lb. filo pastry sheets
1/2 lb. sweet butter, melted

166

Finely chop nuts. Combine filling ingredients in bowl. Cut filo sheets into 4 stacks. Cover 3 with a smooth (not terrycloth), damp towel. Liberally brush first filo sheet with melted butter. Distribute a tablespoon of filling along the short edge. Roll into a cylinder. Tuck sides in to tightly seal. Continue rolling. Brush roll with butter. Place on cookie sheet. Repeat until filo and filling are used. Place rolls 1/2 inch apart on cookie sheet. Bake in 350°F oven 15-20 minutes or until golden. Remove from oven. Immediately place in 10 x 12 x 2 inch pan. Pour syrup over hot rolls. Let stand overnight.

Syrup:
1 cup water
1 cup sugar
1/4 cup honey
juice of 1/2 lemon

Combine syrup ingredients. Simmer, uncovered, 10 minutes. Do not chill.

MEN TALKING
OUTSIDE A TAVERNA
-PATMOS-

GREEK SPECIALTIES

Featured here are various Greek treats which are a little out of the ordinary but so enjoyable one would hate to miss them. A true Greek cookbook would not be complete if they were not included.

GREEK BOW-KNOTS
makes 4 dozen

3 eggs
1-3/4 cups flour
1/8 tsp. salt
1/4 tsp. baking powder
1/4 cup oil

shortening for deep frying
3 cups honey
cinnamon
finely chopped almonds or walnuts for garnishing

170   Beat eggs until light. Sift flour, salt and baking powder together. Gradually add to eggs. Mix by hand if necessary. Turn dough onto flat surface. Add oil, a few drops at a time. Knead to blend. Cut dough into 4 parts. Roll almost paper thin on floured surface. Cut into strips 5 inches long and 1-1/2 inches wide. Melt shortening in deep fryer with basket. (Fryer should be half full.) Heat to 360°F. Fry strips, one at a time. Turn with 2 forks. Shape into bow-knot or twist. Remove when light golden. Drain on paper towels. Heat honey in a saucepan. When bow-knots are cooled, carefully drizzle warm honey over both sides. Lightly dust with cinnamon. Sprinkle with chopped nuts. Bow-knots keep well for months in an airtight container.

Greek Coffee is served in tavernas and after dinner with a glass of cognac. It is made in a small, brass coffee-maker and served in demitasse cups. Greek Coffee is extremely strong and is meant for leisurely sipping. The sign of a well-made cup is the foam floating on the top of the coffee.

4 demitasse cups of cold water
long-handled, brass, 4-cup Greek coffee-maker
4 level tsp. sugar
4 rounded tsp. Turkish coffee

Pour 4 demitasse cups of cold water into coffee-maker. Bring to a boil. Add sugar. Stir until dissolved. Maintain boiling temperature. Add coffee. Stir well. Remove coffee-maker immediately from heat. A foam should appear on the surface of the coffee. Pour a little of this foam evenly into each of the 4 demitasse cups. Then, carefully fill the cups with the remaining coffee. Serve immediately. To gain Greek Coffee's full flavor, sip slowly and allow the fine, thick grounds to settle to the bottom of the cup. Sip until the grounds are reached.

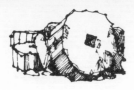

CANDIED GRAPEFRUIT OR ORANGE PEEL

Serve a few of these candied curls in their syrup with a glass of cognac as a sweet, but refreshing dessert.

5 thick-skinned grapefruits or 10 thick-skinned navel oranges
3 cups water
3 cups sugar
172 juice of 1/2 lemon
3 drops of Bergamot oil or 1 tsp. vanilla extract

Using the fine side of a grater, lightly rub the whole surface of each fruit to smooth out the skin and remove some—but not all—of the color. This removes all bitterness. Slice off ends of fruit. With a sharp knife, score the skin into wedges from top to base. Do not cut into pulp. The widest part of wedges should be about 1-1/2 inches as shown in Diagram A. They will taper to about 1/2 inch. Carefully peel away from fruit. Thread a needle with white carpet thread. Use a generous length of thread. Knot 3 inches from the end. Roll each wedge into a tight curl (Diagram B). String curls close together on thread (Diagram C). Put 12 rinds on a thread. Tie necklace strings together until end rinds touch. Place necklaces in 4 quarts of boiling water. Boil, uncovered, 30 minutes for grapefruit and 24 minutes for orange wedges. Rinse necklaces and put in cold water. Refill the pot with water. Bring to boil. Add necklaces. Boil 30 minutes (20 minutes for oranges). Drain. Rinse again in cold water. Combine water and sugar. Add necklaces. Bring to boil. Cook gently, uncovered, until 173 syrup begins to thicken. Test for consistency. Drizzle a little cooled syrup from teaspoon. When it becomes a long, steady stream, it is done. Remove from heat. Add lemon and flavoring. Allow syrup to cool and thicken at room temperature. Remove necklaces from pot. Cut strings. Unlace fruit curls. Place in deep jar with a lid. Pour syrup into jar. Cover. Refrigerate. Serve in small dishes, either chilled or at room temperature.

B.   C.

APRICOT LEATHERS

These delicious strips of candy-like dried fruit are made by pouring a thin layer of pureed apricots onto plastic film to dry in the sun. You will need three consecutive warm, sunny days, a smooth surface such as a table or board, and a roll of clear plastic film at least 12 inches wide and somewhat thicker than ordinary plastic food-wrap. Start early in the morning.

174 12 - 16 very ripe apricots
6 tbs. sugar

Place table in full sun. Stretch plastic film across the surface. Fasten in place with masking tape. Wash, peel and cut away any blemishes from apricots. Cut into small pieces. Place 4 cups apricots and juices in a pot. Sprinkle with sugar. Stir to coat. Place pot over low heat. Heat to just below boiling point. Stir constantly and crush fruit. Remove from heat before it boils. Pour in blender. Blend until it becomes a liquid puree. Cool to lukewarm at room temperature. Pour onto plastic film, spread out into 1/4 inch thick puddles. Make a tent of single-layer cheese cloth over it. Be careful not to touch the puree or let it block out too much sun.

Let dry in direct sunlight for 24 hours. At the end of the first day, slip a cookie sheet under the plastic film. Detach the tape and bring puree inside for the night. Continue sun-drying for 2 more days. Puree is dry when it feels firm to the touch and can be pulled off plastic without sticking. Store leathered fruit sheets by rolling into cylinders. Wrap in plastic. They keep at room temperature for a month and much longer in the refrigerator. To eat, peel from plastic. Tear off a strip and stuff it in your mouth. Apricot Fruit Leathers are chewy, portable snacks or lunch box dessert that provide quick energy.

175

DESSERT PLATTER

The standard Greek dessert is not pastry but a platter of fruits, nuts and cheese.

FRUITS
cantaloupe, cubed
honeydew melon, cubed
176 grapes
apricots
watermelon chunks
peaches or nectarines
pomegranates

NUTS AND DRIED FRUITS
almonds in their shells
pistachios
walnuts in their shells
dried, Calamata crown figs
dried dates
dark and currant raisins
dried apricots

CHEESE
feta cheese, thickly sliced
kasseri cheese, sliced

GRAPE AND WALNUT CANDY ROLLS
makes two 7 inch rolls

40 whole walnuts
2 cans (6 oz.) undiluted, frozen grape juice

10 tsp. cornstarch
confectioners' sugar

Thread a needle with 2 foot length of white, heavy-duty carpet thread. Tie a knot 8 inches from the end. Carefully string 20 walnuts. Tie a knot after the last walnut. Tie thread ends together forming a necklace. Repeat for remaining 20 walnuts. Open 1 can of grape juice. Pour 1/3 cup juice into a jar. Pour the rest of the juice into small saucepan. Heat to boiling. Sprinkle 5 teaspoons of cornstarch into the jar of juice. Shake vigorously. Gradually stir into boiling juice. Cook until thick enough to heavily coat spoon. Remove from heat. Dip one "necklace" into grape juice until every nut is coated. Hang loop in an airy spot. Dip and hang second necklace. Allow to hang 30 minutes. Repeat the whole precedure. Dry necklaces several days until coating is no longer sticky. When dry, repeat dipping. Use the remaining grape juice and cornstarch. Dip necklaces twice. Let hang to dry a week. When dry, snip knotted thread. Carefully pull out. Dust rolls with confectioners' sugar. Slice into 1/2 inch rounds.

TURKISH DELIGHT
makes 2 dozen pieces

3 tbs. unflavored gelatine
1/2 cup cold water
1/3 cup boiling water
2 cups sugar
4 tbs. orange, lemon or raspberry extract
food coloring to match flavor
1/4 cup pistachio nuts, chopped
1 cup confectioners' sugar

179

Soften gelatine in cold water. Add sugar to boiling water. Bring to boil. Stir in softened gelatine. Simmer, uncovered, 20 minutes. Add flavoring and coloring. Pour into ungreased, 8-inch square pan. Add nuts. Stir gently. Chill. When firm, invert onto cutting board. Cut into 1-1/2 inch cubes. Roll in confectioners' sugar. Store in a jar at room temperature. Serve with Greek Coffee, page 171.

INDEX

ANCHORED AT
THE ANCIENT, WALLED
HARBOR OF RHODES.